Organize Your

Work Day
...In No Time

K.J. McCorry

que

800 East 96th Street
Indianapolis, Indiana 46290

Organize Your Work Day In No Time

International Standard Book Number: 0-7897-3333-1

Library of Congress Catalog Card Number: 2004117316

Printed in the United States of America

First Printing: April 2005

08   07   4   3

Trademarks

All terms mentioned in this book that are known to be trademarks or service marks have been appropriately capitalized. Que Publishing cannot attest to the accuracy of this information. Use of a term in this book should not be regarded as affecting the validity of any trademark or service mark.

Warning and Disclaimer

Every effort has been made to make this book as complete and as accurate as possible, but no warranty or fitness is implied. The information provided is on an "as is" basis. The author and the publisher shall have neither liability nor responsibility to any person or entity with respect to any loss or damages arising from the information contained in this book.

Bulk Sales

Que Publishing offers excellent discounts on this book when ordered in quantity for bulk purchases or special sales. For more information, please contact

U.S. Corporate and Government Sales
1-800-382-3419
corpsales@pearsontechgroup.com

For sales outside the United States, please contact

International Sales
international@pearsoned.com

Executive Editor
Candace Hall

Development Editor
Lorna Gentry

Managing Editor
Charlotte Clapp

Senior Project Editor
Matthew Purcell

Production Editor
Megan Wade

Indexer
Erika Millen

Technical Editor
Debbie Gilster

Publishing Coordinator
Cindy Teeters

Designer
Anne Jones

Cover Illustrator
Nathan Clement, Stickman Studio

Page Layout
Michelle Mitchell

Organize Your Work Day ...In No Time

Contents at a Glance

Table of Contents

I Understanding Your Organizational Issues and Goals

II Using Organizational Tools

III Managing Daily Tasks

III Managing Daily Tasks

About the Author

K.J. McCorry is the president and founder of Officiency, Inc., a professional productivity and efficiency consulting company based in Boulder, Colorado, since 1996. Officiency, Inc., specializes in development of paper and electronic office systems for individuals and companies. Ms. McCorry's unique talents in designing systems and coaching individuals in organizational skills make her a leading productivity specialist. Her work in office process simplification has been recognized nationally in the *New York Times*; in the *International Herald Tribune*; in *Mobility Magazine*; and with TV and radio appearances including the Do It Yourself Network and *The Peter Boyles Show*. Ms. McCorry received her bachelor's degree in psychology and international business from Metropolitan State College in Denver, Colorado. She is currently working on her master's in business from the University of Denver. She has been actively involved in the National Association of Professional Organizers (NAPO), currently serving on the Certification Committee. She is the former national Public Relations Chairperson and also served for the Colorado chapter as the Professional Development Chair. She is an advocate of corporate social and environmental responsibility and has served on the board of the Colorado Chapter for Business for Social Responsibility, has served as president of P3 (People, Planet, Profit) of Colorado, and currently serves on the board of the Colorado Sustainable and Environmental Business Association. For more information about Officiency, Inc., consulting services, visit www.officiency.com.

Dedication

To my mother and father.

Acknowledgments

To my professional association, the National Association of Professional Organizers, an association that has supported me throughout my career and whose members have provided me with wonderful business opportunities that have made my business a continual success.

To my professional colleagues, Barry Iszak, Sally Allen, and Elle Page. You all have, through the course of my career, helped and supported me to become my very best. Thank you.

To my computer tech gurus and dear friends, Mike McDaniel and Dave Snow. Your invaluable, gracious computer knowledge and sharing was so appreciated!

To the Que team who encouraged and supported me throughout the book-writing process. Candace Hall, Lorna Gentry, Megan Wade, and Debbie Gilster, thank you for all your guidance and assistance with this book!

To all my clients who shared and opened up their hearts and offices to me. You all have given me great joy in my work.

To the individuals who have always helped me to be a better communicator and writer: Kevin McCorry, Elle Page, Alycia Tulloch, and Leslie Baldwin.

To all my friends who understood my commitment to this book and supported me throughout process. A heartfelt thank you!

To my brother, Kevin McCorry, who has always stood by my side in whatever I have ventured to do. I am blessed to have him as a brother, a friend, and a trusted advisor.

To Earl, Asia, Lakshmi, and Mali, my beloved cats, who sat by my side the entire time! Thank you for your loving spirits.

Tell Us What You Think!

As the reader of this book, *you* are the most important critic and commentator. We value your opinion and want to know what we're doing right, what we could do better, what areas you'd like to see us publish in, and any other words of wisdom you're willing to pass our way.

You can email or write me directly to let me know what you did or didn't like about this book, as well as what we can do to make our books stronger.

Please note that I cannot help you with technical problems related to the topic of this book, and due to the high volume of mail I receive, I might not be able to reply to every message.

When you write, please be sure to include this book's title and author as well as your name, email address, and phone number. I will carefully review your comments and share them with the author and editors who worked on the book.

Email: feedback@quepublishing.com

Mail: Candace Hall
Executive Editor
Que Publishing
800 East 96th Street
Indianapolis, IN 46240 USA

For more information about this book or another Que Publishing title, visit our website at www.quepublishing.com. Type the ISBN (excluding hyphens) or the title of a book in the Search field to find the page you're looking for.

Introduction

I learned about organization mainly from my parents, who were divorced. My mother was the epitome of organization—impeccable order in our house and at her office. She would invite me to come to her office to organize even further than she already was. I would file and organize till the day's end for her office and her colleagues. I enjoyed it immensely and seemed to have quite a knack for office organization. At the time, I didn't realize that every kid didn't organize her mom's office. I thought this was normal kid activity.

I happened to also live part-time with my father, a PhD in psychology, who was the absent-minded professor type. Clutter was everywhere in his household. My father was always looking for that important phone number he had scribbled on the corner of Tuesday's newspaper on the sports section, which invariably I had thrown out or was buried under many other newspapers on the floor. I became my father's personal organizer at the age of 8. We created system after system, until something really worked for him. Between my two parents, I learned how to organize for those who organized naturally and for those who did not think organizationally at all.

In the 1960s, the organization tools and methods we had were limited. Now in the turn of the century, we have so many organizational gadgets, tools, planners, and supplies it is hard to know which ones will offer the most benefit to our specific need. Thankfully, because of our increased organizational tools and knowledge, organization is now not limited to one traditional way. The key is finding the right tool, the right method, the right way for you to be organized.

In my trainings and workshops over the years, I have asked hundreds of participants, "What does organization look like?" Usually the answers come quickly: "a clean desk," "no papers anywhere," "an orderly file system," "a pristine environment." Then I ask, "What does organization feel like?" To that question, I get answers such as "control," "calm," "empowered," "motivated," "light," "free," and "relaxed." My goal in helping you to organize your work day is for you to get yourself organized so that it *feels* right; how your organization looks is less important. In today's information world, it is a difficult task to have a completely paper-free desk and a pristine environment. To create an organizational method for yourself where you feel in control, empowered, and motivated—*that* is organization.

How *Organize Your Work Day In No Time* Can Help You

With the onset of technology, most of us were not prepared to manage our time or information. We had no idea how overwhelmed we would be with the amount of information and electronic data we receive on a daily basis. With data coming at us from email, fax machines, multiple telephones, computers, disks, PDAs and good old-fashioned paper, we all need a way to organize this electronic data and gain control of the technology, information, and time we have.

When will we get it all done? The answer is we will never get it all done. There will always be more email, more action items, more projects, more paper, and more information that will come each and every day. The key is learning how to manage and control this incoming data and information, so that it is not overwhelming. If you feel as though you have lost control to external factors such as your company culture, boss, colleagues, and family, you also probably feel overwhelmed by your responsibilities. *Organize Your Work Day In No Time* offers multiple ways to help you manage your daily workload so you can have control of your projects and schedule and proceed through your day with the confidence that you're getting it all done.

Organize Your Work Day In No Time was created for busy people who want to maximize their time and technology for optimal efficiency. Each chapter guides you through a step-by-step process in multiple areas of your work day so you can become more productive managing your time, managing your data, and managing the structure of your work day. Using the specific and helpful techniques you learn in this book, you will create new habits and gain control over your work day.

This book was meant to help bridge the gap between specific software how-to books and time management books. It teaches you how to use time management principles along with your computer and other organizational tools for maximum efficiency. Most information technology (IT) staff and consultants don't have the time to spend with each and every individual to explain how to customize or best use their computers organizationally. This book steps in where the IT consultants step away, to help individuals learn how to use their time and tools to maximize their efficiency and get the most from their day.

Who This Book Is Written for

Coast to coast, small to large offices, administrator to CEO—most of us have too much to do. American workers are consumed with email, delegations, a constant flow of current projects and new projects, and enormous amounts of paper. With no end in sight, the feeling of finally being done or finished just appears to be nonexistent.

This book is for the average worker in the home or office who would like to experience more control over her work day and computer. The book focuses on using your computer more effectively to maximize your time, but it also offers some good, old-fashioned paper options.

This book is for you if you would like to

- Utilize your system tools more effectively and efficiently
- Learn what it means to "take control of your day" and learn how to do it
- Gain control of your email communications
- Reduce paper and create a paperless filing system
- Create more control with your time and not have urgencies, crises, and interruptions take your day from you
- Learn options for tracking your action list and ensuring you get things done
- Gain ideas on how to maximize meeting time so it doesn't feel like a waste of time

How This Book Is Organized

This book is organized into three parts, and here is what each part contains:

- In Part I, "Understanding Your Organizational Issues and Goals," you'll discover what you want your perfect day to look like. You will gain awareness of how you currently manage your work day and how you optimally would like to manage it. You'll learn the basic principles of organizing and using time management tools to their optimum effectiveness. By the end of Part I, you will have a better vision of your optimal work day and the areas in your life you want to change and simplify.

- In Part II, "Using Organizational Tools," you'll learn how to use your computer more effectively and the secrets to organizing electronic data. You will gain an understanding of how to think electronically and how to maximize the software tools you already have in your computer. You'll also learn how to create a perfect electronic file structure to start the paperless process. You will discover the most useful aspects of using electronic time and contact management software, as well as paper planners. Finally, you'll find out how to protect and manage your electronic data system, so your information is secure and reliable.

- In Part III, "Managing Daily Tasks," you will learn how to manage day-to-day activities. This part includes useful and practical guidance for managing your email and preventing it from overtaking your whole day. You'll learn the basics of how to best manage, track, and organize projects, how to have an effective meeting, and how your participation can make meetings successful. Lastly, you'll learn how to tackle your daily action items, reduce interruptions, and maximize phone communications.

Of course, you're welcome to read this book from cover to cover, which will provide useful tips and suggestions in each chapter. You may also want to read specific chapters whose topics you feel will give you the most organizational help initially. This book will also be a handy reference in the future as your work responsibilities change or as an organizational refresher. You probably will not be able to incorporate all the suggestions immediately, it may take some time. The essence of this book is to help you improve your work day one step at a time, in the areas that you would like to have more control and organization.

We've also placed some important content on our website. Here you'll find the chapter "Managing the Daily Data Deluge," which discusses how to organize your desktop and the scraps of paper that can clutter it and how to back up your data to keep it safe. Another online chapter, "Staying Organized On the Road," teaches you how to plan an effective business trip and manage data while you're traveling. The online content also includes an appendix of websites you'll find helpful as you organize your work day.

To access this online content, go to www.quepublishing.com, enter this book's ISBN (without the hyphens) in the Search box, and click Search. When the book's title appears, click it to go to a page where you can download these chapters.

Special Elements

Throughout this book, you will find a number of tips, notes, cautions, and sidebars that offer additional information related to the current topic. We've flagged five particular types of information with special icons:

Simplify!: This icon marks tips, quotes, and advice for simplifying your approach to time management, organization, and your computer.

Timesaver: This icon signifies shortcuts, workarounds, and general timesavers you can use when approaching various tasks.

Working Partners: This icon signifies product recommendations, books, consultants, and companies offering organizational tools and assistance relevant to a given topic.

Time Traps: This icon marks text that warns you about common time-wasting traps and how to avoid them.

Web at Work: This icon designates references to websites that offer great information, advice, or resources on a variety of topics discussed throughout the book.

In addition, each chapter of *Organize Your Work Day In No Time* offers a series of To Do and You'll Need lists, which clearly itemize tasks you'll accomplish or tools and supplies you'll need in those sections of the chapter. At the end of each chapter, a Summary provides a quick synopsis of what you have learned as well as a review of the action steps suggested in the chapter. Use this element as a quick check of the chapter's information and to determine how best to implement the techniques you've learned in your own work day practices.

Finding "the" Way

All of us are unique individuals, with different habits, methods, and approachs. This book is meant to give you options and different approaches to time and technology management, so you can determine the best way to structure your day and use your computer and other tools more effectively. Not every suggestion is suitable for every person, every type of job, or every type of business. There is no one "right way" to structure organization or time management; use the information you learn in this book to pull together your own "best" way. And, whichever suggestions you want to incorporate into your work day, remember that making any change or acquiring any new habit takes time and commitment.

Part I

Understanding Your Organizational Issues and Goals

Knowing What You Want from Your Work Day

In this chapter:

* Understand what represents a "perfect" work day in your life and how it differs from your current reality

* Learn how to take control of your time and schedule

Today's typical work day looks a little like this: You begin working on email at 8 a.m. Suddenly, it seems, it's 9:30 a.m. and you're rushing to get to that 10 a.m. meeting. Because the client is late and there is too much to discuss, you don't get out of the meeting until 12 p.m. You then grab a sandwich and get back to the office, check email and voice mail, and return messages. The time is now 2 p.m. Your colleague, Sally, comes in to report that there has been a disaster with a client. You leave everything for an emergency meeting to deal with the crisis. At 3 p.m. you settle in to begin work on your to-do list, but your colleague John comes by—he is *so* funny and has a great story to share with you about his weekend. You glance at your watch and it is 3:30 p.m.; you better check email again. At 4 p.m. you look at your list and the papers on your desk and begin doing those small tasks that can get done quickly. At 5:30 p.m. you race out of the office to pick up your kids. At 9 p.m. you check email again because you want to see if anything urgent has happened since you last checked it. At 11 p.m., you lie in bed, feeling exhausted and a bit unsure of what you accomplished that day—but you sure were busy! Does this feel like your day?

In this chapter, you learn how to develop clear and concrete goals for crafting your work days to better suit your needs and working habits. You begin by crafting an outline of what your perfect work day might be. Then, you learn some important techniques for reclaiming ownership of your time, so you can use it as necessary in the course of your working day.

To do list

- ☐ Create an outline of your "perfect" work day.
- ☐ Record activities of your current work day, and calculate how much time you devote to them.
- ☐ Determine current time traps and other issues that prevent you from having the work day you want.
- ☐ Learn how to negotiate "yes" and say "no" when determining how you'll spend your time.
- ☐ Discover when you are most productive during the day, and learn how to use that information to accomplish more throughout your entire day.

Creating a Vision of Your Perfect Work Day

Each person is different in how his "perfect" day looks, but for most of us a perfect day is being able to accomplish our top priorities and having time to build relationships with colleagues and clients, and to deal with unexpected urgencies and crises. Finally, most of us want to go home at a reasonable hour, leaving all work behind and feeling happy, satisfied, organized, and motivated for the next day. Yes, this indeed is a "perfect" day.

Things You'll Need

- ☐ Appointment book, calendar (electronic or paper), spreadsheet software, or other time-tracking tool
- ☐ Pencil, paper, computer, or other materials and equipment used with your chosen tracking document

Sketching Out Your "Perfect Day"

The first step in creating a perfect day is having a clear vision of what you want your perfect day to look like. You can't change your daily work life unless you know how you want it to be and what must be changed to reach those goals. If you don't have a clear vision of how you want your work day to unfold, it will be difficult to take control of external influences that influence your working patterns.

To help you discover your "perfect" work day, I grant you a wish. I grant you the most perfect work day you have ever had. Think about it: If you could have a perfect work day, what would happen in it? What would you accomplish? How long would you work? With whom would you spend your time? And how would you feel at the beginning and ending of that day? To help form a more substantial vision for how you want your working day to be shaped, answer the following questions:

1. What would you accomplish in a perfect day?

2. How many hours would you work daily?

3. Which individuals (both internally and externally) would you further develop business relationships with?

4. How much uninterrupted time would you have during the day?

5. How much time would you spend corresponding by email and phone?

6. What other aspects would make it a perfect day?

7. How would you feel at the end of this day?

Comparing Your Real and Ideal Work Days and Weeks

Now that you've sketched out the elements of your perfect day, you need to determine how it differs from your typical daily routine. To do this, you need to understand how you currently are spending your time. For one week, I suggest tracking what you have done during your day. I know—it feels like tracking what you eat on a diet, and who has time to do that? However, you have to be conscious of what you are currently doing before you can change or even know where you need to change. In addition, most of us aren't out of control the entire day; instead, we lose control of our schedule during certain time intervals. Understanding when those intervals occur and why they are not being used efficiently is essential to changing your habits and taking control of your day.

For one week, at the end of your work day, track in your paper or electronic calendar, what you did during your work day and the approximate time you spent doing it. You can also photocopy the Activity Tracking Table and track your daily activities separately from your calendar. Be as specific as you can tracking your time, and try to account for each hour; include time you spent looking for information, managing emails, and all the interruptions you had during the day.

note I suggest tracking only your work activities and not your personal activities. However, if you would like to know how you spend your entire day, feel free to track all your activities during the day, including personal.

At the end of the week, calculate the total time you devoted to each task or type of task, based on your log. This calculation gives you an estimate of how much time you are currently spending on various activities during the work day and reveals where the majority of your work time is being spent. The following table gives you an example of one way this information could be tracked. In this example, only the hours between 6 a.m. and midnight are tracked, but you might choose to track different periods of time.

At the end of the week, review your log and begin to group similar items together and come up with total time spent. You can group items by your role or responsibility (such as management/supervisory role, sales development, client interaction, projects, and so on), group them by type of action (such as email, meetings, phone, administration, processing invoices/expenses, and so on), or do a combination of both. You also might want to assign percentages for each type of action, based on the total number of hours within the time span you've tracked. The following table shows an example of weekly tracking totals based on some sample types of actions and tracked over a 50-hour work week.

Type of Action	Weekly Percentage	Exact Time (Based on a 50-hour Week)
Email communications	45	22.5 hours
Phone calls	10	5 hours
Interruptions from colleagues	10	5 hours
Weekly meetings	25	12.5 hours
Administration tasks (organizing, mail, filing, and so forth)	5	2.5 hours
Project "A"	5	2.5 hours

The next table demonstrates a weekly tracking record that records activities based on specific roles or responsibilities under which the activities were performed.

Role or Responsibility	Weekly Percentage	Exact Time (Based on a 50-hour Week)
Managing/supervising/HR	20	10 hours
Managing budget/financial resources	10	5 hours
Client development	10	5 hours
Project management of multiple projects	30	15 hours
Administration/planning	25	12.5 hours
New initiative planning	5	2.5 hours

Activity Tracking Table

	Monday	Tuesday	Wednesday	Thursday	Friday
6:00 a.m.					
7:00 a.m.					
8:00 a.m.					
9:00 a.m.					
10:00 a.m.					
11:00 a.m.					
12:00 p.m.					
1:00 p.m.					
2:00 p.m.					
3:00 p.m.					
4:00 p.m.					
5:00 p.m.					
6:00 p.m.					
7:00 p.m.					
8:00 p.m.					
9:00 p.m.					
10:00 p.m.					
11:00 p.m.					
12:00 p.m.					

After you have a clear idea of where you are currently spending your time, your next task is to discover where you would *like* to spend your time during your work week. To make this comparison, complete the following Time Spent: Reality Versus Ideal table. Refer to the weekly tracking total list you just created and use that information to list all your primary work responsibilities in the first column of the Reality versus Ideal table. In the second column, enter the approximation of actual time you spent during the week doing that particular activity or function. Now, think how much time optimally you want to spend doing that particular function or activity; enter that time, expressed as a percentage of your total work week time, in the third column. (The optimal time should be based on the optimal hours you would like to work during the week; if you're currently working 50 hours per week and want to reduce that to 40 hours, take that reduction into consideration when calculating the time you want to devote to each activity in your perfect work week.) For some types of jobs, it is easier to estimate per month and not weekly, so feel free to do that if that works best for you. You also might find that you are over 100% in time allocation, which is okay, too. This is not a perfect science; it is merely meant to give you an idea of how you currently spend your time and where you want to increase or decrease time spent. Those areas or activities for which you want to change the time allocation are the areas on which you should focus your attention. Throughout this book, I provide specific suggestions on how to maximize your time in various areas.

Time Spent: Reality Versus Ideal

Primary Responsibilities and Actions	Percentage of Actual Time Spent During the Week	Percentage of Optimal Time You Would Like to Spend During the Week

Setting Priorities for Change

Review the preceding table to determine which functions have the greatest disparity between the actual and optimal times. These functions are clearly the areas in your job that require time allocation change. If you had problems determining optimal time percentage, you probably don't have a clear idea of the priorities of your job. This could be because you have not clarified these priorities yourself or they haven't been clearly spelled out for you by your supervisor.

Which functions do you do that are essential and important in your department, organization, or business? To clarify priorities, consider having a discussion with your boss and colleagues to get their suggestions for the process. First ask "Which functions of my role bring the most value to the organization, and how much added value could they bring if I devoted more time to them?" This question is very different from merely asking, "Where do you want me to spend my time?" The first question encourages discussion about priorities that are important aspects of your overall position and its value to the organization. The later question can lead to more urgent and immediate issues and tasks. Although both questions can be relevant, the big picture thinking can help tremendously in planning your day.

note If you had a difficult time completing the first two columns, it is probably because you did not have the time to track your weekly activities. In today's world of multitasking, it is hard to determine where we spend our time. If this was the case for you, I encourage you to take the time to track even a day's time, which will provide some clarity to your daily functions.

A number of other books address the process of prioritizing your work day and activities in much greater detail. In Appendix A, "References and Resources," you'll find several references to good books and other resources for more in-depth information on this topic.

Understanding your job priorities is critical to organizing an effective work day schedule. If you are not clear on your work day priorities, the less important tasks and interruptions can eventually take control of your entire day. Keep in mind those responsibilities directly related to your priorities, and plan to devote to them the majority of your work day. These are the key areas to focus on changing.

Identifying Challenges You Face in Taking Control of Your Day

To increase the time you spend on your work day priorities, you need to discover what is getting in the way of doing them in the first place. As you review your outline of a perfect day and the Time Spent: Reality Versus Ideal table you created, can you determine what is stopping you from having that perfect day? What are the things that are preventing you from achieving that ideal state? Is it interruptions? Is it your boss or colleagues? Is that there is too much to do and no clarity on priorities? Is it the 100 emails you receive daily? Is it that you just don't have enough time to do everything you need to do? Go ahead, and list all those challenges and obstacles to having your perfect day in the following space (or use another sheet of paper or word-processing document, if necessary):

1. _____
2. _____
3. _____
4. _____
5. _____
6. _____
7. _____
8. _____
9. _____
10. _____

To gain control of your work day, you have to address each and every one of these challenges and obstacles. Keep them in mind as you continue to read this book. Each chapter provides you with specific options, tools, and suggestions to help you combat most of the obstacles you have listed. You can use the ideas and techniques you learn from these examples to address other types of specific challenges you face in gaining control of your work day schedule. This list provides a roadmap for change and improvement as you implement the ideas you learn in this book.

Learning to Negotiate Your Commitments

How you make daily agreements is essential to taking control of your work day. Discovering which types of things, actions, and people you can—and should—say *yes* to is necessary if you want to keep your work day activities focused on your job priorities. How often do you say *yes* when you really mean *no*? It probably happens more frequently than you think. Why? In our work culture, being a good person and team player typically means never saying *no*. It also feels good when we say *yes* to helping others; saying *no* can be difficult, especially when we're dealing with a boss, colleague, or client. Yet, your work time is limited, and therefore you must learn to negotiate the *yes* along with the *no*.

Learning to say *no* or *yes* is really learning the art of negotiation. The definition of *negotiation* is "a discussion intended to produce an agreement." During negotiations, there is communication of what works best for both sides—there is not a blind *yes* or *no* to any negotiation. Think of a time when someone had to say *no* to you or renegotiate a commitment. What aspects of that *no* made it okay? How was it communicated? What options or other solutions were presented? What reasons made it feel okay? Taking each view into account and coming to a mutual agreement and solution is the way in which we negotiate and make agreements with others.

Let's say your boss continually delegates to you action items that are really not in your realm of responsibility and that jeopardize your ability to complete your own

action items. In addition, you view these action items as having low impor
value to the organization. What do you do? How do you say *no* to your boss.

Maybe, instead of saying *no*, you simply need to negotiate a *yes* response. Begin by asking your boss for more information. Clarify the scope and importance of the task being delegated. Communicate your top priorities and let your boss know your understanding of where your priorities lie. Ask if you are truly the best—or only— individual in the organization who can assume these tasks. Lastly, if you must say *yes*, suggest a date you feel is reasonable for completing the extra duties and negotiate to mutual satisfaction.

With each and every request for your work time commitments, there should be clear negotiation on the appropriateness of the task and time it will take place. Thus, you are not really saying *no*; you are merely negotiating how you say *yes*. When you have clarified your priorities and understand the obstacles that get in the way of those priorities, then negotiating the *yes* becomes vital to managing your time.

In print, on the Web, and through other media, you can find a lot of information about negotiation and how to develop negotiating skills. If you want to learn more about negotiation skills, I encourage you to read one of the leading books on negotiation, *Getting to Yes*, by William Ury (a full reference for this book appears in Appendix A).

Matching Your Activities to Your Working Style

When do you work best? Is it morning, afternoon, or evening? When is the optimal time for you to do certain activities? Most of us spend our morning doing email, and that might be the right choice for you, too. If your time zone puts you behind others you're working with or you're working on a high-priority project that involves regular email communication, a first-thing check might be essential. But many people dive into email immediately when reaching the office simply out of habit. If you're one of the latter group, is reading and responding to email really the best use of your morning time? Only you can determine the answer to that question.

But think about a situation in which you had a huge project to do—something that would take you between 2 and 3 hours to accomplish. If you could choose the ideal time of day to work on that project, what time would you choose? Logically, you would choose the time of day when you have the best concentration and focus, a time when there is less activity in the office, or a time when you feel most energized and creative. By determining when these times occur during your day, you can better determine how to structure your activities to maximize your productivity.

If you're better able to focus and be creative during the morning, then your morning time might be better spent reviewing documents or working on important projects rather than email. If Friday afternoons are slow in the office and an ideal time to work on a particular project, then block out Friday afternoons for project work. Think about which types of activities you perform that require your full attention and focus, and consider altering your daily and weekly schedule to reflect these optimal times.

DEVELOPING A PERSONAL MISSION STATEMENT

A personal mission statement is a phrase or sentence that captures what you want to do and, ultimately, what you want to be in the world. It is intended to be a statement of purpose and goals. Developing a personal mission statement can help you make the decisions and determine the priorities that shape your work life.

To develop a personal mission statement, first, brainstorm a list of events, items, people, and beliefs that are important to you. This can include past successes or actions, people you live and work with, as well as your personal and business goals, values and beliefs. Then, review that list and look for commonality within all the words or phrases that you wrote down. Finally, with those commonalities in mind, create a sentence or short paragraph that sums up the list. That sentence or short paragraph is your personal mission statement. This exercise isn't easy; it can take time to ponder such important issues. You may need several days or weeks to really come up with your personal mission statement.

Once you have developed a mission statement, review it periodically to remind you of what is important to you in your life. You also may find that you want to rewrite your mission statement as time progresses.

There are a few books about how to write mission statements. I recommend the book, *The Path: Creating Your Mission Statement for Work and for Life*, by Laurie Beth Jones.

Franklin Covey also offers an excellent online wizard to help discover and develop your own mission statement. Log on to www.franklincovey.com and click the Mission Statement Builder. Once completed, this wizard downloads to Microsoft Outlook users a task list to help begin the action steps toward living your mission statement.

Web at Work

To do list

- ☐ Begin to change the over-worked paradigm.
- ☐ Control your computer; don't let it control you.
- ☐ Consider what you would do with free time.

Taking Back Your Time

Americans are overworked. According to research by the Economic Policy Institute based in Washington, the average American worker has added 199 hours to her annual work schedule from 1973 to 2000. That averages out to be about 5 additional work weeks per year for each working American. Americans are also reducing their time spent on vacations. According to a study in 2002 commissioned by Expedia.com, Americans forfeited 175 million days of vacation time that was due to them that year. Instead of enjoying the vacation time they'd earned, those Americans "donate" it to their employers—a whopping $20 billion of it.

As I said in the Introduction, you will *never* get it all done. "Never, not no how," as the Wizard of Oz would say! Yet, we continue to work ourselves, sometimes to the point of serious illness or death, to try to get it all done. We have lost the understanding that the time we have is *our* time. Instead, we tend to operate under the impression that our work time is under the influence and power of external forces beyond our control and we must continue to strive endlessly toward the impossible goal of getting it all done.

I have a secret. The secret is that we don't have to operate that way, if we don't want to. The choice is ours. Is it difficult to change a paradigm of an entire work culture? Absolutely. Consider this: If we all don't begin to change being overworked and overwhelmed, the change will never happen. Our children will grow up expecting to be overwhelmed and overworked and assuming that's how working life should be. And you, the reader, will be reading another time management book in the future thinking it will provide the salvation to change your life. Your salvation in this effort is completely and entirely up to you. You have to want the change, and then you have to determine *how* you will change. I am not suggesting that we all quit our jobs and never work again, (although, for some, that might be a perfect day)! What I am suggesting is changing *how* we work and *how long* we work.

What's Making You So Busy?

As the computer microchip increases in size and speed, we seem, as humans, determined to keep up as well. The notion that the Technology Age would free us from work has in fact produced the opposite. We seem to have doubled and even tripled the work that we do on a daily basis. In a study conducted by Franklin Covey in 1998, 58% of the respondents felt that technology advances had actually given them *more* time. I tend to think technology has reallocated our time, not necessarily reduced it.

With the advent of personal computers on everyone's desks and access to the Internet, an enormous amount of data is at our fingertips every second of the day. In Theodore Roszak's book *The Cult of Information: The Folklore of Computers and the True Art of Thinking*, he says, "It is estimated that one weekday edition of today's *New York Times* contains more information than the average person in seventeenth-century England was likely to come across in an entire lifetime." It is also estimated that it takes 24 months for information in the world to double in size, according to David Shenk in his book *Data Smog*. He also cites that more information has been generated in the last three decades than in all the previous 5,000 years put together. That is a lot of information!

Busy-ness across the nation is prevalent in this Technology and Information Age. It wasn't anyone's fault or intent—it just happened. However, it is up to all of us to change the paradigm. It won't change itself. Unfortunately, technology will only get faster and we will continue to be inundated with more and more information every day. The expectations of getting it done quicker and faster will continue to rule our days. We do not have to live in one of those blockbuster science-fiction movies where the computers take over the world. We have the power to turn the computer on and turn it off.

The computer has certainly enhanced and dramatically changed our work life. The computer is a tool, a tool that can be managed, a tool that can be useful, a tool that can be organized to help manage time and data to increase efficiency. As you read this book, you will learn about the electronic options available to help you manage and organize your information. It is important to remember that we should control our computers, and not the other way around.

THE TAKE BACK YOUR TIME MOVEMENT

Take Back Your Time Day is a national movement that addresses the overworked, overwhelmed, time-starved American culture we currently live in. The movement encourages and educates how individuals can create more time for families, friendships, communities, volunteerism, and oneself. The initial idea stemmed from the Simplicity Movement that has gained momentum in the last decade. Individuals who have become tired of working hard, tired of not having enough time with their families, tired of being in debt and paying bills, and tired of the pressure to upgrade to the latest and greatest consumer goods have begun questioning Americans' workaholic mentality. Being overworked is affecting our health, our families, our communities, our environment, and our nation, as a result.

If you would like more information about Take Back Your Time Day, go to www.timeday.org. Consider reading the book *Take Back Your Time*, edited by John de Graaf. This book is a compilation of respected authors, counselors, philosophers, physicians, and academics who discuss how the American culture has focused and encouraged overwork and overtime. It offers practical suggestions for individuals, companies, and governments to change the overwork/time paradigm.

How to Take Back Your Time

If you had all the time you wanted or needed, what would you do with it? This question in some respects is the most important of all. If you didn't have to do what you are currently doing, what would you do? If that question is hard to answer, there is really no incentive, no motivation, for you to change your current time habits. You can't take back your time if there is no compelling reason to do so.

Have you ever had a free 10 minutes for some reason, and you didn't have access to your computer, didn't have any reading material, didn't have anyone to talk with, and didn't have your cell phone? Panic set in because you wondered what you would do with that entire 10 minutes! Your mind began to tell you instantly how unproductive you were going to be in the next 10 minutes if you did not find something immediately to do. You began to look around and search for something to do. Think! Think! There must be *SOMETHING* you could do. Relief only set in when the 10 minutes had passed, and you were on to the next action, as planned. We have become so consumed and programmed to fill time that we do not know what to do with any free time we might have.

We are tiring ourselves out. We are trying to work longer and harder and, in the end, we are experiencing burnout, depression, and sickness. It's not a very productive work day when that happens! It appears Americans are forced to change time habits only when sickness strikes or family separations occur. Taking back your time is about being proactive with your time allocation, before serious repercussions happen.

I encourage you to consider and give serious thought to what you would like to do if you had free time. Contemplate it; write it down in your diary or planner. When life feels frazzled, go back and review this list. This is why you want to get your time back, this is why you want to be more organized and productive, and this is why you want to have control of your work day.

According to Steven Covey, author of *The Seven Habits of Highly Effective People*, "Time management is not the ability to squeeze more hours into the day. It is not the capacity to triple-book oneself in an effort to get more things done. It's not about getting more things done at all. It's about accomplishing the important." Your dreams, your wishes, your aspirations, whether personal or work related, are all important to accomplish.

It has been said before in many time management books, seminars, and lectures, and it should be said again: We all have the same 24 hours in a day. No more, no less. What we choose to do with those 24 hours in the day and how we spend them is entirely up to us. We do have choice in how we spend and plan our day, week, month, and year. We do have choice in how we manage our daily tasks and make agreements. Once choices have been made, commitment to managing and organizing the process are next.

Summary

Perhaps realizing our perfect day seems almost impossible. If so, it's because most of us are unsure of how to change the daily external obstacles that seem to get in our way. This chapter has helped you learn ways to focus not on what is impossible, but on what is possible. You have learned that it is possible to overcome barriers and obstacles. It is possible to spend time on those functions and activities that we have deemed important. It is possible to negotiate tasks to someone else or to a later date. It is possible for you to Take Back Your Time and begin to move in the direction of how you ideally want to spend your time during your work day. This is called "creating your perfect day!" Here's a list of the important tasks you've learned in this chapter. Use this list to construct your own action plan:

- Track all your actions during the day for an entire week and discover how you spend your time.

- Determine what the priorities are in your day and create an optimal time allocation of your responsibilities.

- Develop your negotiating skills and learn the art of saying *yes* and making agreements.

- Consider why you want to have more time.

In the next chapter, you learn some basic organizing principles along with ideas for using basic time management tools.

Organizing Basics

2

Many organizing systems have been developed to help individuals with organizing their time. Essentially, all organizing tools and practices can be related to three very simple organizing principles: consolidation, categorization, and creating a home. These organizing principles can be applied in all areas of your office and personal life. No matter what you are organizing, thinking through these principles before developing a system will help you think through designing your own organized system. In this chapter, we address each organizing principle in more depth and focus on the aspect of how it relates to information, data, and time.

Time-management tools are the map or plan of how you intend to manage your work life. They come in both paper-planners and electronic organizers. Products such as Franklin planners, day timers, Palm Pilots, Blackberrys, and even basic spiral notebooks are some of the more common time-management tools on the market today. Some form of time-management tool is essential in managing your day effectively. There are so many tools and supplies that can help us with time management that it can be difficult to know which one might be the best for you. This chapter discusses which time-management tool might be right for you and your job. It also covers the basic premises of using time-management tools effectively.

To do list

- ❑ Purge unnecessary information and begin to consolidate your data.
- ❑ Consider assigning designated areas for your information.
- ❑ Determine whether a paper planner or an electronic time-management tool is best for you.
- ❑ Be consistent with tracking your information in your time-management tool.
- ❑ Carry your time-management tool with you to meetings and out of the office.
- ❑ Use only one calendar, if possible.

Things You'll Need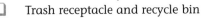

- ❑ Trash receptacle and recycle bin
- ❑ Current time-management tool

The Three Principles of Organizing

The three principles of organization are consolidating, categorizing, and creating a home. These principles can be applied to any area of organizing in your office or home. With any organizing system you develop, it is important to apply these three organizing principles. The value of applying the principles enables you to find what you need, when you need it. In the following section we discuss each principle in more length. In later chapters when we discuss specific suggestions about organizing systems, we will refer to these principles and how they apply.

Principle 1—Consolidate

If you have ever moved your office or home, you realize how much stuff you really have. It is estimated that we use 20% of what we possess only 80% of the time. So, why do we keep it all? You guessed it—because we think we might need it! As with other important things, letting go of information can be difficult because we are not sure of its value in the future. Thus, our tendency is to keep it all. But saving every scrap of information that comes our way makes it difficult to access the information we really do need. Who has time to sort through everything to find a particular piece of needed information? Thus, one of the first principles to organization is consolidating our information and data to weed out the stuff we don't need and group the data we do want to keep.

Purging Unnecessary Information

To begin consolidation, you need to purge information—including paper and electronic documents, reading material, business cards, and email—that you do not need or use. Purging is the most difficult aspect of office organization for some individuals, and it can even bring the whole organizational process to a stop. Many people worry about destroying information that they or a colleague might later need. Don't let the "I might need it" fear get in your way when you begin to organize your data and your office. The key to overcoming your reluctance is to address your concerns directly and analyze whether they are justified.

As you begin to make decisions about what information to keep, think about how long in the future you want to keep particular types of information—one year? two years? three years? longer? Begin to develop your own guidelines for retaining your office records, and use them to create a simple table or spreadsheet. In one column list the document/data type, and in a second column record the length of time you believe you should retain that information. Review and update your record retention document annually so you have a useful guide for future purges.

tip

Some companies have record retention policies developed for certain types of information. Find out whether your company has a record retention policy. This can help you create your own retention guidelines and you help during the purging process. Refer to the sidebar "Online Resources" for more information on records retention guidelines.

Although you might find it easy to determine what you need to keep and what you need to purge, inevitably you will run across a few pieces of information that stump you. If you answer *yes* to any of these questions, you probably need to keep the item:

1. Is the information related to a current action item or project that you are working on?

2. Is this information past history that would be valuable for future related communications, projects, or planning?

3. Do you use this information or item on a regular, day-to-day basis?

4. Is this information current and up–to–date?

5. If you really needed this information, are you sure there is no other place you could get it easily, such as from a colleague or from your email records, hard drive, or the Internet?

6. Is the information required to be kept by government legislation compliance or company retention policies?

ONLINE RESOURCES FOR RETENTION POLICY GUIDELINES

A records retention policy provides clear guidelines on how long you should retain various types of documentation. Often companies develop their own internal document retention guidelines based on industry guidelines and standard company practices. If your company does not have a records retention policy, the following are several online resources that provide helpful information about developing records retention documents and policies:

American Records Management Association (www.arma.org)—ARMA is an organization of records management professionals. Its site contains a wealth of information about paper and electronic records management.

Iron Mountain (www.ironmountain.com)—This company provides services for record and information management. If you go to its resources section, you'll find a wealth of information of articles and white papers about compliance, legislation, and how-tos on record management.

Online Organizing (http://www.onlineorganizing.com/ExpertAdviceToolboxTips.asp?tipsheet=24)— Provides a general record retention list for personal and small business documents.

The Sarbanes-Oxley Act (www.sarbanes-oxley.com)—This act outlines government-mandated compliance for the financial industry for recording and maintaining all data associated with financial audits and reviews.

Health Insurance Portability and Accountability Act (www.hipaadvisory.com)—The HIPPA Act describes the government's record-retention mandates for the medical industry, as it applies to all data related to medical information on individuals. This link also provides other legal retention guidelines for other industries: http://www.hipaadvisory.com/regs/recordretention.htm.

Association of Corporate Counsel (www.acca.com)—The ACC has developed an extensive records retention manual called "Records Retention InfoPak" for corporations and legal offices. This can be downloaded free if you are member of the ACC.

Other Items for Consolidation

Beyond purging information you don't need, consolidation also involves pulling together and grouping information you intend to keep. In upcoming chapters, we'll talk about organizing your electronic data. But in the early phases of your work day organization, you may benefit most from organizing the paper documents and data scattered about your office. You can most easily begin this process by sorting through and categorizing the types of information you have on paper. Here are pieces of information you need to consolidate in preparation for organizing your work day and your paper or electronic time-management tool:

- Action items and tasks you need to complete
- Notes regarding phone calls and voice mail messages
- Addresses, contact information, and business cards
- Reading information
- Meeting notes
- Information that needs to be entered as data into data-management or other types of software
- Reference and filing
- Projects

This data currently might be consolidated in your paper planner or software, or it might be scattered on tablets, Post-it notes, message pads, and so on. To begin bringing order to the paperwork in your office, you should consolidate each type of data in one pile or location. As you sort through the paper piles on your desk, begin to make a separate pile for each information category. When you are done, you might want to put these separated piles temporarily into a manila file folder to keep all those loose pieces of paper together. We will refer to these sorted piles and learn more about how to organize and categorize all these types of information.

 As you work through the process of organizing your office and work day, I encourage you to trust your decisions. If you are hesitant about beginning the process and feel you need more help getting started, consider hiring an organizing consultant or coach. An organizing consultant can discuss your information needs and uses and ask you specific questions that make the organization process easier. Organizing professionals can also help you customize systems for your unique needs. To locate a professional organizer near you, go to the National Association of Professional Organizers website at www.napo.net.

Principle 2—Categorize

After you have consolidated your data, the next step is to begin categorization. The *Sesame Street* generation often practiced the game of One of These Things Is Not Like the Others. In essence, this is the same process you'll be going through when you categorize your information. Categorizing your information is the process of determining the relationships between pieces of information. After you determine to which common group, topic, or classification information belongs, you begin to develop a categorization structure. Categorizing your data makes it easier to access and helps you build connection and organization within your office.

You categorize your information in keeping with the way you think and the type of job you have. Choose categories that are natural for you to remember and understand, so your documents and other information will be easy to find and access. For example, if you have paper documents that all relate to a particular project, you might choose to consolidate and categorize those documents by the project name. If you associate your projects more readily with the client name, rather than the project name, you should categorize the documents related to your projects by client name. You might categorize all monthly expense records within a single group called Expenses, or you might group them by month or type, as in January or Travel. Each way is perfectly useful and appropriate, depending on how you want to access and refer to this information. In Chapter 4, "Creating the Perfect File System," we discuss in more detail how to create your own category structure and ways to create subcategories.

Principle 3—Create a "Home"

The third principle to organization is assigning a *home*, or a designated place for all your objects, documents, and information. This home can be within a desk area, filing cabinet, time-management tool, or computer software. After you have consolidated and created categories, you will have a better idea of which type of space or structure you will need to serve as a home for your various types of information.

Choose homes for your information based on how often you access the data; information you access most frequently should be closest to you, while data you rarely need to access can be located in a less-convenient spot. Ideally you want the information you access most often within arm's reach.

The accessibility of your information's designated home can determine how well you maintain the data in that location. Your data and information must be easy to access and retrieve; otherwise, you are unlikely to put information in its designated home. Maybe you want to put a paper document in its proper file but aren't willing to leave your desk, walk three steps to the right, lift up your arm, pull open a drawer that is difficult to open, find the file, and then put the information inside the file (which is too full to hold anything more, anyway). Or, maybe you don't want to take the time to click through five or six icons and files in a directory to access a file for updating electronic data. So, instead of going through all that effort, you'll decide to put that information right there on your desk, where it stays and becomes slowly buried under lots of other inaccessible information.

Updating and maintaining your data is easier when that data is easy to access and retrieve. To determine when you need to reallocate your space or purchase new supplies, equipment, or software for storing your information, you need to be able to access and evaluate the current

> **tip** When choosing a home for your information, consider your habits. If you have a habit of writing miscellaneous notes near the phone, consider putting your paper planner or handheld near that location. If your habit is to take your phone with you but not your handheld planner, consider purchasing a combination phone and handheld. Sometimes adjusting systems to your habits can be easier than changing your habits.

storage situation. Easy access makes for easier and more reliable maintenance. You can simplify the task of keeping your records up-to-date and in their proper home when you locate those homes wisely.

Maintaining Your Organizational Plan

Even though you've consolidated, categorized, and found homes for all your information, you haven't finished with your organizational tasks. Eventually, the home areas you have designated for your information will become full. When that happens, you can resolve the problem by choosing among one of the three organizational principles you've just learned:

- You can purge and consolidate the information stored in the area to free up some of its existing space.
- You can subcategorize the information and create additional subsection homes within the current category.
- You can seek another larger location. For example, say you have a nice in-box tray on your desk but the tray overfills quickly, either because you receive so much information or you have a difficult time purging and sorting on a regular basis. When your inbox becomes full, your colleagues begin to create new in-box areas, placing documents on your chair or keyboard, taping them to your door or computer monitor, or placing them on the floor in front of your door. When this situation occurs, your in-box's home is not working. Using the three options outlined earlier, you can fix this situation by consolidating your inbox and reviewing its contents regularly, by subcategorizing and creating two or more inboxes to hold different types of information, or by finding a larger inbox tray.

THERE'S NO PLACE LIKE HOME

Often when homes get full we are tempted to create a temporary resting place for documents, often in a nice open space, such as on a bookshelf, on a desk, on the floor, or even in an empty drawer. You might find yourself thinking, "I don't have time to find another home, so I'll just put it right here in this open space where only I know it will be—it's perfect because I can see it and I know exactly where it is!" But if you give in to that temptation, these wide open spaces soon become cluttered with miscellaneous information and you'll need to find another area to store information, and then another area, until your office falls into a state of disorganization. To keep your office clean and manageable, and to avoid wasting time hunting for information you've left in some "easy-to-find" location, always remember the golden rule of office organization: Everything has a home and *that's* where you need to store it!

Not only do you need to designate locations for your information, but you also must begin the habit of sticking with the home you have designated. That two seconds it takes for you to open the software and enter a bit of data or stand up and file a document will save you hours—yes, hours—of time in the future when you want to access that piece of information. You have to reprogram your mind to acknowledge that you don't have the time *not* to put everything in its home. Throughout this book, we discuss multiple types of designated areas for information. You need to choose the homes that will be most accessible and easy for you to use.

Choosing a Time-management Tool

A time management tool is a way to track your day-to-day activities, contact information, tasks, and other reference information you use on a daily or regular basis. Some individuals track this type of information solely paper-based in a multitude of forms, including planners, sticky notes, tablets, and paper calendars. Others track this type of information completely electronically, with the use of contact management software, handhelds, and other data storage software. The third group uses a little bit of both, which we discuss in more detail in Chapter 6, "Hardcopy: Using a Paper Planner."

THE EVOLUTION OF TIME-MANAGEMENT TOOLS

From the 1940s to the 1970s, time-management tools consisted of a desk calendar, a card Rolodex, and a separate tablet for a to-do list. Then in the 1980s we upgraded to standard paper planners where information of calendar, contacts, and action items were consolidated into one notebook. These planners eventually became customized, enabling us to determine which type of calendar view, address book, and notes pages worked best for our needs. The paper planners could, however, be large and cumbersome, making it difficult to find information within them. In the late 1990s, developers created small, portable, and easy-to-use electronic planners, freeing us from the need to lug around oversized paper planners. Today, a wide variety of contact and personal information software and hardware have become the new time-management tools. We now have the capability to sort, find, and track information in both paper and electronic formats.

To do list

- ☐ Consider your working style.
- ☐ Compare the pros and cons of using paper and electronic planners.
- ☐ Choose a planner type that's right for you.

Matching Your Tools to Your Personality and Style

Now that you have a multitude of time-management tool choices, which choice is best for you? This depends on who you are, what you do, your personal working style, and the type of information you need to track. Analyzing this information can help you determine which type of time-management tool is best for you.

The following table offers some typical profiles of paper and electronic planner users:

	Paper Planner Users	Electronic Planner Users
Who are you?	Like to work with paper-based information. Mistrust and are uncomfortable using computer systems.	Find paper difficult to manage and organize. Feel at ease on computers and using software.
What do you do?	Computer use is infrequent. Action items are immediate or solely paper-based. Responsible for one primary responsibility or project. Limited follow-up with others required. Minimal meetings and have no need to coordinate with other colleagues.	Computer use is frequent. Required to keep electronic calendar for officewide viewing. Responsible for multiple projects. Extensive follow-up with clients and colleagues. Frequent meetings that need to be coordinated with other colleagues.
Where are you located?	Usually in an office but not located at a desk or near a computer. Travel in a vehicle during most of the day.	Always at a desk and near a computer. Travel frequently and carry a laptop. Attend multiple meetings.
What type of information do you need to track in your planner?	Minimal meetings and appointments. Minimal contact information. Minimal phone calls and voice mail messages.	Lots of contacts and business cards. Multiple meetings and appointments, which can change on a daily basis. Multiple projects.

Using Paper-based Planning Tools

Paper planners are useful tools for individuals who do not need to track a large amount of data or a large number of appointments. Others, who have primary contact with colleagues in the office and limited need for outside contacts, also find it easier to keep the few business cards they have in a Rolodex or paper address book. Those whose jobs are largely made up of repetitive daily tasks might have little need to track action items, either on paper or electronically. Then, there are those who just prefer the tangible aspect of paper and writing information down physically. The simple act of writing down a piece of information can make the information easier to remember.

Paper planners are also recommended for individuals who do not feel comfortable using a computer or don't have ready access to a computer on a daily basis. Individuals who are not good typists also find it difficult to quickly enter data electronically and therefore like the ease of handwriting. Learning new software can be tedious and time-consuming; thus many people find it easier to stay with a paper-based system. And those individuals who have lost electronic data due to crashes and viruses also are less apt to keep their important information in an electronic planning system.

If you've had difficulty using a handheld, you might consider staying with a paper-based time-management tool. You might find handhelds to be awkward to use and just not worth the time to figure out. Writing with a stylus or the small keyboard takes a steady hand, and it can be more time-consuming to enter data than merely handwriting it yourself. Also, because the screen is small, it is difficult to see data in larger content views, such as a monthly calendar view. The following table summarizes the pros and cons of using a paper planner:

Pros and Cons of Using a Paper Planner

Pros	Cons
Ability to see calendars more visually.	Heavy or bulky, which could discourage you from carrying it with you.
Require no electricity to operate.	Awkward to change calendar appointments and meetings.
No software to learn.	Time-consuming to track action items and reenter to new date or page.
Handwriting information can be quicker than entering it electronically.	Handwritten data can be difficult to read and view.
Handwriting information sometimes helps with memory recall.	No search and find utility, making it difficult to find historical data quickly.
Portable.	

Using Electronic Planning Tools

Using electronic planners can be highly effective for individuals who track a large amount of data and would like to become "paperless." Electronic planning tools are also convenient for storing and tracking data that changes numerous times. It is far easier to change the recorded date and time of an appointment within an electronic planner than it is to erase and rewrite the information numerous times in a paper planner. Electronic tools are also good for tracking contact information (such as names, addresses, phone numbers, emails, and so on) and historical notes. Individuals who have multiple projects, action items, and future related tasks often find it easier to track that information electronically than on paper.

Electronic tools are good for individuals who like handhelds and gadgets, find them easy to use, and aren't frustrated by entering data or viewing information. If you're comfortable working with software and adept at using a computer, you might prefer to use an electronic time-management tool. Skilled typists often prefer entering information electronically, eliminating problems with hard-to-read handwriting.

Electronic planners also are light and easy to carry. Paper can be time-consuming to organize and heavy to carry. A handheld device can be easier to carry in a suit pocket or purse than a standard-sized paper planner; therefore, you might be more likely to carry it with you. The following table lists the pros and cons of using an electronic planner:

Pros and Cons of Using an Electronic Planner

Pros	Cons
Light to carry.	If not handheld, limited portability.
Easy to change appointments and meetings.	Difficult to see weekly and monthly calendar views.
Easy to find and track historical data.	Small text is difficult to see printed or on the computer screen.
Ability to convert data to different electronic forms.	Reliant on electricity to operate.
Ability to see data in multiple views.	More important to have a backup system in place.
Ability to store a large amount of data.	Need to be proficient at software to maximize effectiveness.
Ability to have reference books and material stored on handhelds.	

Following the Rules of Time-management Tools

For effective time-management tool use, whether paper or electronic, here are some basic rules that make using them more effective:

- **Use the tool**—Often we purchase a great new handheld or a customized paper planner but don't use them. They just sit in the box or package, waiting for us to take the time to learn how to use them. If you think you are unlikely to learn new software, or don't have a clear idea of what you will use a particular tool for, be cautious of purchasing these tools. After you determine the best time-management tool for you, take the time to learn how to use it. Learning any new tool can be awkward and take some time to assimilate as a normal daily habit. Developing (good) habits takes patience and persistence. Neither a paper planner nor an electronic tool will work automatically. It takes you, the user, using it!

- **Be consistent**—Apply organizing principle number three and create a home for your time-management tool both in and out of your office. Locate your tool where you will most often need to use it—for example, on your desk or near your phone or computer.

Make a habit of always putting your time-management tool in its home. Doing so will save you time you might have spent trying to locate the planner, and it will make using it easier.

Also be consistent in the way you use your planner. For example, if you determine that you will write all your action items in your paper planner in a separate designated section, be consistent and always write in that area. The same consistency is recommended for tracking your contacts, calendar, and daily notes. If you have a habit of tracking in multiple areas and multiple tools, searching for information can become frustrating. Be consistent with the tool you use, where you place it, and where you track your day-to-day information.

- **Take your tool with you**—Unlike a portable planner, your brain stays with you at all times. If you don't carry your time-management tool with you, you'll spend a lot of mental energy trying to remember information until you get back to your office and can record it in your time-management tool. Trying to remember all the data that comes to you is distracting—and impossible. Inevitably you will forget data as time moves forward. Carrying your time-management tool with you enables you to record information as it comes to you, freeing your mind to deal with other tasks at hand.

 Don't try to sidestep your time-management tool by recording information on napkins, receipts, or other odd pieces of paper that just happen to be handy. These bits of paper are easy to lose, along with the data you've recorded on them. Thus, make the effort to always take your time-management tool with you.

Summary

Understanding and implementing the three basic principles to organization is key to long-term organizational success. With all systems and information you develop, it is important to take into account these principles and apply them. This chapter has helped you make a decision about which type of time-management tool you'll use.

You also learned how to determine whether a paper-based or electronic tool, or a combination of both, will be better for you, based on your job and individual work habits. Whichever tool you choose, be consistent in your use of it.

In this chapter you learned:

- Purge unnecessary information and begin to consolidate your data.
- Consider assigning designated areas for your information.
- Determine whether a paper planner or an electronic time-management tool is best for you.
- Be consistent with tracking your information in your time-management tool.
- Carry your time-management tool with you to meetings and out of the office.
- Use only one calendar, if possible.

In the next chapter, "Joining the Electronic Age of Organizing," we talk about the benefits of being organized electronically. You also learn some of the basics of technology to help you feel more comfortable about storing your data electronically. Lastly, we talk about how to create one primary system for all your data, whether in electronic or paper form.

Part II

Using Organizational Tools

3

Joining the Electronic Age of Organizing

When computers first came on the scene, many office workers figured that they would be the "magic bullet" for managing paper. Experts predicted that computers would create the paperless office we all had dreamed of. Today, most offices are anything but paperless, though computers have become essential in ways none of us could have predicted. In this chapter, you learn a number of methods for using electronic data management to make your workday more organized and easier to manage.

Today, most office workers maintain an enormous amount of electronic data in various forms within multiple software applications. Because there is so much information in today's work world, it is vital that we begin to think of how we want to organize our electronic data in addition to organizing our paper documentation. In this chapter, you learn how to create one world of information and data and begin the process of organizing your electronic data.

Although organizing your electronic data is an important step in organizing your work day, computer maintenance is an equally important part of that process. When your computer isn't working or your data has been destroyed, your productivity might stop completely. To avoid the chaos and

In this chapter:

* Learn about the "paper-less" trend and what you can do to support the movement

* Discover the benefits of creating parallel electronic and paper filing systems

* Learn the benefits of becoming more organized electronically

* Understand the basics of your computer system

lost time that can result from computer malfunctions, the average worker needs to maintain at least minimal knowledge of the workings of computers. By learning your computer's basic specifications and capabilities, understanding its file management system, and managing its basic maintenance tasks, you can keep both your computer system and your day-to-day work day organization running smoothly and efficiently.

Making a Case for Using Less Paper

Everyone is talking about the "paperless" trend happening in America, when in fact, it is just the opposite. America's consumption of paper has doubled in the last 10 years—a period that marks the rise of computers as essential office tools. According to the book *Myth of the Paperless Office* by Abigail Sellen, a company's use of email has produced a 40% increase in paper consumption. Hewlett-Packard did a study in the year 2000 that cited U.S. workers print on average 32 pages from the Internet per day. U.S. paper producers consume approximately one billion trees every year. This amounts to roughly about 735 pounds of paper annually for every American office worker! According to the paper industry, it expects that paper consumption will double by 2050. Clearly, we are not in a paperless trend.

RECYCLED AND TREE-FREE PAPER RESOURCES

We need to reduce paper consumption and help purchase recycled and alternative paper. Unfortunately, recycled paper isn't widely used even though it is available at large office supply stores. According to the Recycled Paper Coalition, less than 20% of office waste paper is recovered for recycling. The good news is that the American Forest and Paper Association in 2002 created a nationwide goal to recover over 55% of the paper consumed. However, they need everyone's help in continuing to support recycling efforts in their offices and communities. For more information about paper recycling in your office, contact Inform, Inc. (www.informinc.org), a nonprofit organization based in New York that helps develop recycling systems in the workplace.

If you would like to reduce paper waste, consider purchasing recycled and tree-free paper. Here are a few companies that provide alternative paper products:

Green Earth Office Supply (www.greenearthofficesupply.com)—Offers a wide variety of office supplies that are earth friendly and sustainable

Green Field Paper (www.greenfieldpaper.com)—A paper company that offers a wide variety of alternative options, including paper made from hemp, cotton, and recycled paper

Office Depot (www.officedepot.com)—Offers recycled content paper and is a leader in green office supplies

Recycled Products Purchasing Cooperative (www.recycledproducts.org)—A nonprofit organization that sells recycled paper and alternative paper

In addition to the environmental impacts, paper is time-consuming to manage. Record keeping constitutes more than 90% of all office activity. According to a study done more than 10 years ago, U.S. companies file approximately 120 billion sheets of paper annually. Of that paper filed, over 80% is never referenced again!

After you print out a hardcopy, you then have to deal with it by sorting, organizing, filing, and eventually purging the document. As we are inundated with, print, and accumulate more paper, the time spent managing it mounts, as well. The task of managing paperwork becomes overwhelming, and too often, the paper piles up around us on our desks. If you reduce the number of documents you print, you can cut down on one major source of paper overload, help create a more organized office and work day, and save yourself considerable time.

Paper is expensive, too. How many square feet of space is devoted to filing cabinets in your office? Multiply that figure by the cost you pay for each square foot of your office space. If you fit the national average, then 80% of that figure is your cost for storing information you don't use. With real estate prices only going up and the size of offices becoming smaller, it is important to maximize our office space. If you reduce the paper pileup, you can save money and maximize space in your office.

To begin to create that paperless office, we all need to reduce our paper consumption and get organized electronically. Moving to electronic organization methods is about changing your thought patterns and realizing that you don't need a hard copy of every piece of information you use. Managing electronic data is much easier and less time-consuming than managing paper. To move toward a paperless organization system, you need to have basic knowledge and control over your electronic data, using techniques you learn about in this and the next few chapters.

To do list

- ❏ Gather and record information about your current organizational system.
- ❏ Determine exactly how you want to access your information.
- ❏ Explore alternatives for categorizing your data.
- ❏ Categorize and subcategorize information to create a master outline structure.

Moving into One World of Data

To be certain of where your data is located, it is important to create one world of data. This means matching all your information systems to follow one master outline or structure. Currently, you might have one system for your paper files, a different system for email files, another system for electronic files, yet another system for tracking websites, and perhaps a database or two for collecting other types of information. When you receive paper and electronic information, that information might be filed in three to five different locations and categorized and subcategorized by different topic names within those systems.

When you use the "one world of data" approach to information management, you think of all your data as one entity, and no matter what form that data is in, it is stored in the same category or structure within all your information systems. Using this approach, all your information systems will be parallel to one another. That, in turn, simplifies filing and retrieving information, no matter where within the system it is stored.

note There can be (and often will) be slight deviations within your master filing system. Information that you receive mainly in only one form, such as email, may require additional subcategories in your email structure but not in your paper structure. We discuss this more in later chapters when we discuss how to create your paper filing system, electronic filing system, and email filing system in more detail.

Things You'll Need

- ❑ Current organizational information
- ❑ Pencil and paper/word-processing software

Creating a Master Outline Structure

Back in high school English class, you probably were taught to create outlines of book reports and other papers. One of the challenges of that process was to determine the basic components of what you would write before you wrote it. Creating a master outline for information is much the same process. You need to determine what you have to organize before you organize it! Most office workers use the opposite approach for storing information—as information comes, they find a place for it somewhere in their system. Filing new information becomes frustrating when there's no designated file location within a structured system. When you create a master outline structure, you have already determined where you will file all the data you receive, in whichever form you receive it. The structure makes filing *and* finding the data easier.

Determining Organizational Levels

Take a moment and think about your job and all the data you receive, including paper and electronic documents, mail, email, contacts, meeting notes, research, books, articles, and information from the Internet. Review how you are currently sorting and organizing all that data, and write down all the systems within which you have organized each of these types of data. Record your current method of organizing the data and list the names of files, categories, subfiles, and subcategories you have created within each system, as shown in Figure 3.1. You will use this list to help you create your master outline structure. Notice that in some areas your information is consistent within systems and in other areas there are differences.

Ideally, with your master outline structure you want to create at least three or four outline levels. The first level will be the primary categories of information. Your primary categories could relate to the company organization chart, your department organization chart, your primary areas of responsibility, associations, or major projects. Sometimes the primary categories are a combination of all those. Take a look at the list you created earlier, and highlight the primary categories that seem to be common throughout all your systems. Ideally, you should have 10–15 primary categories, but this number can vary from job to job.

After you have created your primary categories, you need to think about how you want to subcategorize each of them. Here are the standard ways in which to subcategorize information:

- **By subject**—Documents are arranged by subject name or category, similar to topics in phone directories and in libraries.
- **By name/Alphabetical**—Documents are alphabetically arranged by names. For example, this could be names of clients, suppliers, or employees.
- **Geographically**—Documents are arranged by geographic location, such as by continent, regional area, country, state, county, or city.
- **Numerically**—Documents are arranged by numerical order. This could be by an assigned job number, an invoice number, a project number, a client number, or an employee or Social Security number.
- **Chronologically**—Documents are arranged by date order. This can be done by annual or fiscal year, by month, by quarter, or by date.

When determining how you want to subcategorize, consider first how you want to access your information. Which topic, name, or word do you first think of when you are looking for that piece of data? For example, assume you have a primary category called Clients that contains all your client information. When you need to access client information, you might first identify clients by the state where they're located, then the name of the company, and then maybe the type of project you did for them. So, your primary category would be Clients, the second tier would be by geographic region or state, the third tier would be by name or company name, and the fourth tier would be by subject or project name. The subcategorization you choose will be different for each primary category.

Current Paper System

Paper file system is currently in alphabetical order by name of the Manila file. Filenamaes include

Budget 2003
Budget 2004
Awards
ABC Project
Expense Report Form
Haines-Gregory Personnel File
Health Insurance
Logo
Performance Reviews
Sales Projections 04-05
Staff Meeting Notes (all years in one file folder)
Terry-Jane Personnel File
Training Information
Travel Information
Website Information

Current Email System

There are a few email file folders I created, but I rarely use them.
Our IT system usually deletes emails after 90 days so
I keep most of my emails in my inbox folder.
The email file folders do have are

Client A
Personal
Sales Projections
Travel

Current Electronic System

Current electronic file system documents are organized primarily by name of the program.
Subfiles include

Word
Excel
PowerPoint

More than 100 electronic documents are not in subfiles and just
below the subfiles in one long list underneath the My Document folder.

Reference Material

Current reference material including books, magazine articles,
conference notebooks, and miscellaneous papers are located on the bookshelf.
Most reference material is sorted with one category per each shelf. Categories include

Management, Leadership, General business books
Industry information
Financial information
Travel guidebooks, maps, and city information

When planning your subcategory structure, look at the paper and electronic filing structures in your own office and company. Ask your colleagues how they organize certain categories. You might discover a way to subcategorize that you had not thought of before. You also might want to be consistent with your office structure and create subcategories based on the officewide system.

For the most part, when you purge data, you do so because it is outdated. Thus, when possible and applicable, try to subcategorize data by years. This helps you in the future to purge outdated data very quickly without sorting through individual files and documents. It also makes archiving electronic data much easier.

Drafting an Outline

Below is a sample master outline. Yours will vary depending on your business and job. In some cases, the primary categories in the sample structure might be subcategories under a different primary category you have created. If you feel you don't have enough information to create a second level, try to determine how, if the data increased in size, you would want to subcategorize it. This helps you in the future as you accumulate more data within that particular category. Some categories don't require a third or fourth level. Determine levels based on the data you receive and the way you use that data.

In later chapters we discuss how you can customize your master outline structure to each of your information systems such as paper, email, electronic, and your contact database. For right now, though, you are just thinking of all your data as one world of data and developing the structure as if it were all in one big pile in the same form.

Here's a sample you can refer to when drafting your own master outline. In this example, each item is preceded by a number that represents its level within the outline structure:

    1: Administration (second tier by subject)

        2: Forms

        2: Staff Meetings (third tier by year)

            3: 2003 Staff Meetings

            3: 2004 Staff Meetings

        2: Policies and Procedures

1: Clients/ Customers (second tier by client name)

    2: Company A (third tier by project number)

        3: Project 1

        3: Project 2

    2: Company B

    2: Company C

1: Financial (second tier by subject)

    2: Budgets (third tier by fiscal year)

        3: 2003 Budgets

        3: 2004 Budgets

    2: Sales Projections (third tier by annual year)

        3: 2004 Sales Projections (fourth tier by month)

            4: January 2004

            4: February 2004

1: Marketing (second tier by subject)

    2: Logo

    2: Marketing Material

    2: Website

1: Personnel/HR (second tier by person's name)

    2: Haines-Gregory

    2: Smith-John

    2: Terry-Jane

1: Personal Information (second tier by subject)

    2: Awards and Recognition

    2: Health and Medical

    2: Performance Reviews

    2: Résumé and Recommendation Letters

    2: Training

1: Press and Media (second tier by fiscal year)

    2: 2004

    2: 2005

    2: 2006

1: Projects (second tier by project number)

    2: #111 (third tier by subject of project components)

        3: Budget

        3: Statement of Work

    2: #222

    2: #333

1: Reference (second tier by subject)

    2: Budgets and Financial Reference

    2: Leadership and Management Reference

    2: Travel Reference

    2: Trends in Industry Reference

Consolidating Systems

Organizing principle number one—consolidation—is a key factor in moving into one world of data. Ideally, you need to consolidate all your existing data into one location. This will help you in the organizing process.

You might have electronic files on your personal C drive, floppy disks, CD-ROMs, and the shared server system. To make your electronic data easier to manage, consolidate all your data onto one drive before you begin to organize it.

The same consolidation is recommended with your email. You might have multiple accounts with different Internet service providers that you check in two different email programs. Consolidate by managing multiple email accounts from within the same email program. Microsoft Outlook, in particular, can be set up to receive multiple email accounts to be downloaded into one central inbox. This consolidation can save time and avoid the hassle of needing to check two different accounts in different email programs.

Paper files have a tendency to become fragmented because you have one paper system that is outdated and has not been purged in a few years, one paper system that was left by your predecessor, and one paper system that is current information. Ideally, it is best if you consolidate all three systems in one area and file system.

 tip Simplify your passwords and have a logical, systematic method for selecting each. Most passwords now require numbers and letters, so try to create combinations of the same ideas. For example, if your pet's name is Earl and your mother's birthday is in June, you can do multiple combinations of those ingredients, such as 06Earl or Earl061945. Try to catalog your passwords with the company contact information, or consolidate them all in one confidential file area.

BENEFITING FROM ELECTRONIC ORGANIZATION

Because as much as 90% of your documentation might be received in electronic form, it is much easier and cheaper to organize, file, and access your information electronically. Here are the key benefits to keeping your data electronically;

• **It creates easier access**—The find and search features in all software are more extensive than they used to be and are only getting better. You also don't need to stand up and walk anywhere to get to your data; you can manage and access all of it right there from your desk chair.

• **Data is managed more efficiently**—Managing paper is time-consuming. On the other hand, if you receive an electronic document via email, you merely have to perform several clicks, which take less than 30 seconds, and the document can be filed immediately.

• **It's cheaper to store and archive data electronically**—Using average rates, it costs about $600 per year to store 20 standard filing boxes. With 100 pages of documents roughly equal to 1MB, one file box of paper is approximately equal to about 23MB of memory. Hard drive memory for a standard 40GB drive costs about $200 in 2005, which equals about a 5¢ cost per 1MB. Thus, storing one file box electronically has a one-time cost of about $1.15. Clearly, an incredible cost savings. As technology advances, electronic storage will only get cheaper.

• **Electronic data is easier to take with you**—When you go on a business trip, it's difficult to pack up your filing cabinet in boxes, carry them to the airport, ship them with you, take them to the hotel, and have them there just in case you need them. With the majority of your data in electronic form, you can easily take a large amount of data with you. Even if you don't have a laptop, there are now multiple ways to carry electronic data, including USB storage devices, which can hold up to 512MB of memory on a small keychain-size device.

Understanding the Technology of Electronic Organization

Understanding the basics of your computer system is important in order to organize your electronic data effectively. In today's office culture, IT staff are constantly backlogged helping employees and sometimes aren't always available. Knowing the basics of computer maintenance and troubleshooting can help you maximize your time and utilize your computer more efficiently.

To do list

- ☐ Familiarize yourself with your computer's type, size, and so on.
- ☐ Determine drive and server allocations.
- ☐ Learn about your system's file management software.
- ☐ Create a list of basic computer maintenance tasks, and plan to perform basic computer maintenance on a regular basis.
- ☐ Learn basic troubleshooting tasks.

Things You'll Need

- ☐ Computer manuals and system summary information
- ☐ Contact information for your IT department
- ☐ System Tools utility for your operating system
- ☐ Antivirus software

Getting to Know Your System

Whether you are attempting to fix a problem yourself or contacting the IT department for help, you need to know the configuration of your computer and system for the best results. Located on most PCs and Macs is a system Information window that provides information about your operating system, type of computer, and size of memory. Learn where your system summary is on your computer. On most Microsoft PC systems, select Start, Programs, Accessories, System Tools, System Summary.

Most office computers are networked to a central computer, usually called the *server*. Larger organizations sometimes have multiple servers to manage all their computers. Usually each individual employee, or department, has designated space to use on the server. Sometimes, the IT department creates the appearance of a separate drive, such as the H drive or I drive, to designate this space on the shared server system. The server computer systems are generally backed up daily by the IT department. Again, contact your IT department for this information, record the information, and keep it handy for future reference.

Each computer also has a separate hard drive, usually called the C drive. This C drive is where all software programs are installed and run. The C drive also can store My Documents, Internet favorites, and email attachments. The C drives of individual computers are usually not backed up by the IT department. If you are storing documents and information on your C drive, you need to find an alternative method of backing up your data. For more information, see the online chapter "Managing the Daily Data Deluge." This can be found at www.quepublishing.com.

Located on most computer systems is a standard file manager software, where you can view and organize all your files. On Microsoft systems, it is called Windows Explorer and is usually identified as the file folder icon with a magnifying glass on top of it.

FIGURE 3.2

Shown here in Windows XP is Microsoft Explorer open to a user profile file folder located under Documents and Settings.

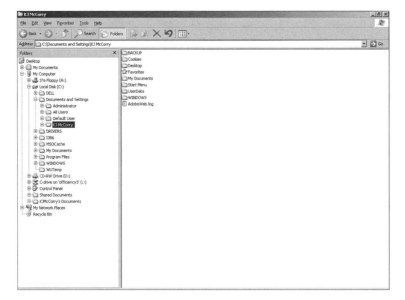

In this program you can also locate system information. Click to highlight a drive name (a drive usually has an alpha letter next to it); then right–click to produce a pop-up menu of options. Select Properties from the menu and the Properties dialog box appears, containing information about that drive, including its size, function, and available space. If you right-click a folder and select Properties, the folder's property dialog box shows you the size of that particular folder. File manager programs typically are the easiest places to find, organize, and access data. You don't have to remember with which software a document was associated—you merely have to click the document you want. It automatically opens the software program.

tip

Keep important computer and hardware data such as serial numbers, product ID numbers, tech support phone numbers, email settings, and ISP account settings all in one document and in an accessible paper file. This is important, especially when your hard drive crashes.

Performing Basic Computer Maintenance and Troubleshooting Tasks

Sometimes a significant portion of your work day is spent trying to troubleshoot problems with your computer and other equipment. Knowing basic troubleshooting and maintenance techniques for your computer and other hardware devices can come in handy. Better yet, by performing basic computer maintenance tasks, you often can avoid problems altogether. Performing basic troubleshooting and maintenance saves you time, and thus serves as an important part of your work day organization plan.

note This section lists some basic computer maintenance processes for most computer systems. Check with your IT department and your computer consultant to see whether there are any others that you should perform regularly based on your particular computer system.

Disk Cleanup

You should clean up your hard drive annually by removing nonessential files, such as temporary files, cookies, deleted files, and downloaded files. With Microsoft operating systems, you can clean up your hard drive by selecting Start, Programs, Accessories, System Tools; then click Disk Cleanup. It automatically scans your C drive system for files that could be deleted. Review the Disk Cleanup options, recommendations, and files before clicking OK.

caution If you are not in the habit of saving your email attachments to another location, be careful with deleting the temporary Internet files. Depending on your system configuration, that is usually where email attachments are stored. Take a quick look before you delete anything.

Defragmentation

Defragmenting reorganizes the space in your hard drive and increases the efficiency of the system. It is important to defragment your hard drive monthly to increase the efficiency and speed of your computer.

To perform a defragmentation on Microsoft PC systems, select Start, Programs, Accessories, System Tools; then click Disk Defragmentation. Click your C drive and click OK. Mac systems don't usually have built-in defragmentation tools, so you must purchase one from a third party, such as Norton Utilities. Follow the directions for using your defragmentation tool, and be sure all your documents are closed when you perform this process. It can take up to an hour to perform a defragmentation, depending on your system.

Virus Scan

To help protect your computer from worms, Trojan horses, and other computer attacks, it is important to update your virus scan software weekly and run a full system virus scan monthly. Most virus scan software has an automatic schedule built in that performs a full system update and virus scan automatically. If you are not able to update your virus scan software, you might have to renew your monthly subscription to perform this function.

To date, most viruses do not affect Macintosh computers, though some do. Norton (www.norton.com) and McAfee (www.mcafee.com) are two well-known manufacturers of third-party antivirus software.

Troubleshooting Tips

Although everyone can benefit from learning a few basic troubleshooting techniques, this knowledge is particularly important for those who work at home (and don't have the benefit of an IT department). Depending on your computer issues, here are a few basic troubleshooting techniques to try before calling in a computer technician:

- Turn off your computer and reboot completely. If your computer is not responding at all, hold down the power button until it turns off.

- Check all power cords and make sure everything is plugged in correctly. Sometimes, cords get slightly pulled out and cause a malfunction.

- For PC systems, press Ctrl+Alt+Del (all at the same time) and click Task Manager. Highlight the program that seems to be malfunctioning and click End Task. This shuts down that particular program; then you can reopen it.

- Update your virus scan software and then perform a full system virus scan. If your computer identifies a virus, call your computer technician immediately.

tip When you get your computer, copy machine, or printer serviced, take the time to be present and learn the troubleshooting steps your professional performs. Don't hesitate to ask questions that will help you understand the basic processes for maintaining your equipment and troubleshooting other problems.

You can learn more by taking a computer class at your local community center or adult learning center. Also, take the time to find a reliable computer consultant who can assist you with computer issues and problems as they arise. Contact the Independent Computer Consultants Association (www.icca.org) or your local telephone directory to find someone in your area.

note Whether you are working on a PC system or a Mac, the same organizing philosophy applies to both. Throughout this book, most of the suggestions are geared for PC systems but can be applied in the same methodology to Macs. Appendix A, "References and Resources," contains a brief glossary of technical terms that might be useful to review and reference.

COMPUTER ERGONOMIC TIPS

It is important when working on a computer every day to have proper placement to avoid injuries. Here are a few computer ergonomic tips:

- Purchase an antiglare filter for your computer screen.
- Purchase a footrest for underneath your desk. This can be beneficial if you experience back pain.
- Consider mounting a keyboard tray under your desk for more comfortable typing.
- Consider purchasing a wrist rest or ergonomic mouse to prevent hand and wrist disorders. Also take a break from typing every hour to relax your hands.
- Place your monitor about 28" away from you.
- Consider using document holders that hold documents vertically. This can help with neck pain.

For more information about computer ergonomics, go to one of these websites:

- Healthy Computing (www.healthycomputing.com)
- International Ergonomic Association (www.iea.cc)
- U.S. Department of Labor (http://www.osha.gov/SLTC/ergonomics/index.html)

Summary

Creating matching filing systems for both paper and electronic data makes it easier for you to sort, access, and organize information. By reducing the amount of paper you print and saving your data electronically, you will reap enormous savings in time and expense. To feel comfortable with electronic data storage, however, you need to understand a few computer basics. If you have difficulties sorting out exactly how your computer works, you might benefit from taking a class or talking with your computer consultant or IT system manager.

In this chapter we learned how to

- Reduce paper consumption and avoid printing. Keep information in electronic form and rely on your computer for your data.
- Create a master outline structure of all your information and data. Use this outline as the basis for organizing all your paper and electronic systems.
- Perform regular computer maintenance to optimize your computer system.
- Take a computer class to understand the basics of your computer, troubleshooting, and maintenance.

In the next chapter, "Creating the Perfect File System," we discuss in detail how to create an electronic and paper file system that is easy to use and maintain.

Creating the Perfect File System

The average worker loses one hour a day looking for misplaced documents. Organizing your electronic documents is just as important as organizing your paper documents. Having paper and electronic systems work seamlessly together is an optimal way to have your office organized and avoid wasting time searching for lost documents.

As we discussed in Chapter 3, "Joining the Electronic Age of Organizing," there are numerous benefits to keeping your information in electronic form. Creating a paperless office can be a diffi cult challenge when your electronic directory is not organized and you don't trust your electronic filing system. In this chapter we discuss how to create the perfect electronic filing cabinet for all your electronic documents.

Because the amount of paper in offices has doubled in size, we also discuss how to create an effective paper filing system that parallels your electronic structure. It is important to become aware of why you keep paper and think about how long you really need to keep hard-copy documents. This chapter explains how to create and maintain an effective paper document filing system that meshes well with your electronic filing system. You also learn about scanning documents and how to use effective maintenance techniques to keep your filing systems in order and increase your productivity.

To do list

- ☐ Develop an electronic filing structure that parallels your master outline.
- ☐ Select the best location for storing your electronic files.
- ☐ Create electronic subfiles when you have more than 30 documents in a file folder.
- ☐ Determine the best location for historical electronic documents.

Creating an Electronic File Structure

Some electronic computer files are stored in an organizing structure that has virtually no rhyme or reason. Sometimes electronic documents are stored under a single file folder, which is the equivalent of storing all paper office documents in one file cabinet drawer, with no hanging files or Manila folders to categorize them. Stashing all your documents within a single folder—whether electronic or paper—makes using the system difficult and time-consuming.

It is best to create an electronic file structure based on the master outline you created in Chapter 3. That master outline is based on a topical outline structure, which simplifies the process of filing data in paper and electronic formats. Electronic documents and their hard-copy versions are filed under identical names, making information stored within the two systems easier to file and retrieve.

Things You'll Need

- ☐ The master outline structure you created in Chapter 3
- ☐ Computer and file management software of your choice

Choosing a Storage Location

Before creating your electronic filing structure, you need to determine where you want to store your electronic data files on your computer. Don't worry about where you store your program files; those files usually stay on your computer hard drive in

their original folder and location. If you work in a company on a networked system, most likely your IT department gave you a personal file folder or drive space on the server. This might be the best location to store your electronic data because the server systems are usually backed up nightly. Some individuals prefer to keep their documents on their hard drive, or C drive, and not on the network server because they find it is easier to access and more reliable. If you select this option, be sure to choose and follow a backup plan, as explained in the online chapter "Managing the Daily Data Deluge." Go to www.quepublishing.com to download this chapter.

If you have a standalone computer, you have the option of storing electronic files on the computer's hard drive—most people use the C drive. Many computers today have 40GB or more of memory available, and many have two hard drives (typically, a C drive and D drive). If your computer has two hard drives, you can keep your programs on the C drive and your data on the D drive. If you have only a single hard drive, you can store both data and programs on that drive.

It's best to set up your file structure within one master folder; this makes backing up and moving stored files easier. If you choose to store your data on the C drive, you might want to use the existing folder called My Documents to hold your electronic file structure. If you choose to store documents on the network or a different drive, you might have to create a new folder called Data or My Documents to begin your electronic file structure.

Organizing Your Files

Review the master outline structure you created in Chapter 3, and create the same outline structure in your hard drive. The electronic file system you create will probably have more subcategories than the structure you initially created in the master outline, depending on how much electronic data you currently have. Create your electronic file system first, before you begin to reorganize the electronic documents you want to file within it. With your system in place, you easily can drag and drop files into the appropriate file folders, without stopping to create a new file folder.

If you're working on a PC, you can use the standard Windows Explorer program to organize files. Select Start, All Programs, Accessories, Windows Explorer to open the program. Or for a quick shortcut, you could right-click the Start button and select Explore to open Windows Explorer. For Mac-based systems, just click the Mac Drive icon on your desktop.

When organizing electronic files, you should use the double-pane view. To do this in Windows Explorer, click the Folders icon, as shown in Figure 4.1. On a Mac, select View, Column View.

Folders icon

FIGURE 4.1

If you click the Folders icon in the Microsoft Explorer toolbar, you can work in a two-pane view.

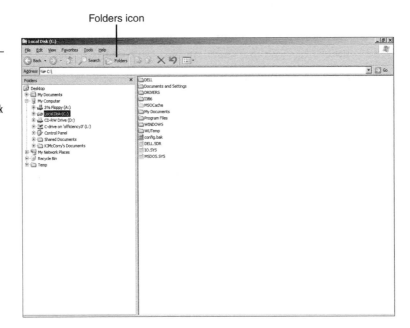

Creating New Folders

In the double-pane column view, the left side lists all the primary files and drives and the right side lists the contents of a highlighted folder. This view simplifies organizing electronic files and makes dragging and dropping files and documents from one pane into another easy. The Mac OS X system opens multiple columns to the right as you click file folders.

Electronic file folders are designed and viewed in an outline structure sorted in alphabetical order. To create a new file folder in Windows Explorer, highlight the file or drive in which you want to create the new folder (such as My Documents or Data). In the toolbar, select File, New, Folder, as shown in Figure 4.2. Initially, the file folder is named New Folder and the name is highlighted; type the new filename to change the name of the folder. If you accidentally click out of the new file before you have typed your filename, just right-click the new folder and select Rename from the context menu.

FIGURE 4.2

Here, a new folder is being created in the My Documents folder; the My Documents listing is highlighted, which opens that folder so a new subfolder can be added.

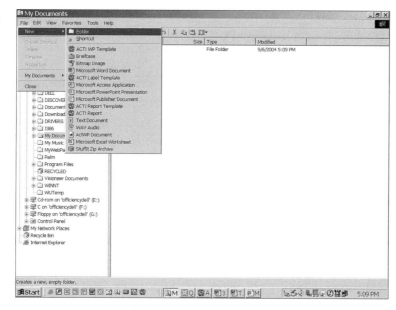

Create your master outline structure electronically by creating new file folders for all primary and subcategories. Create as many subfolders as is necessary to reproduce the master outline structure you created in Chapter 3. Figure 4.3 shows a sample electronic file structure based on a master outline. If you accidentally create a subfolder in the wrong major folder, you can click and drag the misfiled folder to the correct master folder (make sure the correct master folder is highlighted before dropping it).

FIGURE 4.3

This electronic outline structure mimics the structure of the sample master outline discussed in Chapter 3.

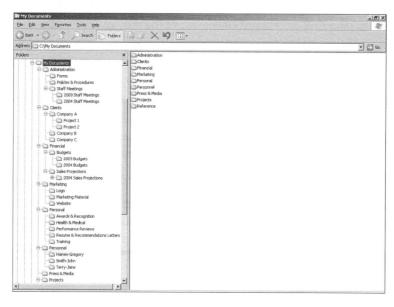

To create file folders on a Mac, select File, New Folder, as shown in Figure 4.4. To create subfiles, you must open a file folder window and repeat the same process.

FIGURE 4.4

Here, in Mac OS, a new folder is created within the Documents folder. After a new subline is created, the Mac OS system automatically shows the new subfolder in the right column.

Adding Files to Folders

After you have created your electronic filing system, you do not have to return to Windows Explorer or the Mac drive to add files to existing folders or to create new folders. You can create additional file folders in the Open or Save As command window in any Microsoft Office program. This is especially useful if you are saving a new document in the Save As window and want to file it under a new file folder name.

To create a new folder using the Save As command for PCs, follow these steps:

1. With the document open that you want to save in the new folder, select the Save As command in any Microsoft program; the Save As dialog box opens.

2. The Save In text box at the top of the dialog box lists the name of the folder in which the file or new folder will be saved. If the listed name isn't correct, use the drop-down arrow to select a new location.

3. In the toolbar at the top of the Save As dialog box, click the Create New Folder icon, as shown in Figure 4.5. The New Folder dialog box opens.

4. In the New Folder dialog box, type the name of the folder you want to create; the new folder appears in the proper master folder. Double-click the new folder so that it appears in the Save In text box.

5. Be certain that the name in the File Name text box is correct; then click Save.

You can create a new folder while working in Microsoft Office software for Macintosh by using the New Folder button in the Open or Save As command window, as shown in Figure 4.6.

FIGURE 4.5

Using the Save As command for PC systems, you can create a new file folder.

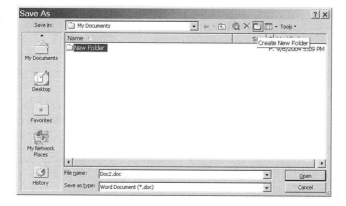

To save a new document in a new file folder on the Mac OS X system, follow these steps:

1. Select the Save As command in any Microsoft program.

2. Click the text box just below the Save As text box and select the location of the new file folder.

3. In the lower-left corner of the Save As dialog box, click the New Folder icon.

4. Type the name of the folder you want to create; the new folder appears in the proper master folder.

5. Click the new folder, so that it appears in the text box below the Save As text box.

6. In the Save As text box, make sure the correct name of the file appears. Select the Append File Extension command if you want to send the document to a PC user. Click Save.

FIGURE 4.6

In the Save As command for Mac systems, you can create a new file folder by clicking the New Folder button located in the lower-left corner of the window.

In either the Open or Save As window, you can delete, rename, or create shortcuts with documents or file folders. To do so, right-click the document or folder you want to move, rename, or otherwise refile; then select the appropriate command from the context menu that appears (see Figure 4.7). The only function you must perform in Windows Explorer or the Mac Drive windows is the movement of files and documents into one another.

note With Mac systems, the file extension is not automatically added to a filename when you save the file. If you need to send attachments to PC users, be sure to click Append File Extension so that PCs can open the attachment.

Copying and Moving Files Among Folders

To move documents into the correct file folder, open the file management program and, with the files and the correct folders displayed in Folder or Column view, highlight the document or file folder you want to move. Then click and drag the document to the correct file folder.

If you do not have a two-pane view in your file manager software, you must highlight the document, select Cut or Copy, open the correct file folder, and paste the document into that folder. If you drag and drop files or documents within the same hard drive, the files and documents are moved to the new location. If you drag and drop files or documents from one hard drive to another hard drive, the files are copied, not moved.

FILE ORGANIZATION SOFTWARE

Here is a list of some specific software that can help with file organization. Most of these programs function very similarly to Windows Explorer. Although you needn't use file management software to create or organize your electronic files, those programs typically offer additional functionality you might find useful in organizing and maintaining your electronic records.

Each listing also includes a web address where you can find more information about the product or order it online:

* **File Wise (www.filewise.com)**—A PC-based file manager and database software that helps you organize electronic documents; it can be used to record filing and storage locations for hard-copy documents and other stored objects. Used this way, File Wise can serve as an all-in-one information organizer.

* **Universal Explorer (www.spadixbd.com)**—This PC software actually replaces Windows Explorer as your file manager. It offers the capability to view documents without opening them and to compress documents into Zip files.

* **FileQuest (www.piquest.com)**—This PC software enables you to view file folders in multiple panes, thus making viewing and organizing files and documents easier.

* **PowerDesk (www.v-com.com)**—This PC software offers the feel and look of Windows Explorer but provides the capability to simultaneously search over multiple drives. You can also compress files and enable password protection, if desired.

* **Enfish (www.enfish.com)**—This PC software integrates with Microsoft Outlook and enables you to save emails and other types of documents in the same electronic file structure. It also indexes and cross-references documents and files.

* **Utility Dog (www.probabilityone.com)**—This Mac file management software is a fully functioning file manager and can be used on any 8.1 OS or higher system.

Creating Subcategories for Your Documents

When a folder has more than 30 documents in it, subcategorize the folder contents by creating subfolders. Refer to your master outline and the subcategory structure you developed there; then create the subfiles based on that structure. For example, if you have a file folder titled Staff Meetings with more than 50 documents of meeting minutes for the past four years, create chronological subfolders by year and store each year's minutes in the appropriate subfolder. This simplifies the process of finding meeting minutes from the current year and purging older minutes.

> **tip** To view file properties such as size and location, right-click any file folder and select Properties (for PC systems) or Get Info (for Mac systems). To move up or down quickly within the file system hierarchy in Windows Explorer, click the Back, Forward or Up buttons in the Explorer toolbar.

Create the subfolders using the same process you used to create the master folders. Begin by highlighting the file folder within which you want to create the subfolder. For Mac users, you must first open the folder window to create subfolders.

To view the subfolders you have created in PC systems, double-click the master folder listing in the left pane; the subfolders automatically appear in the right pane view, as shown in Figure 4.8. Alternatively, you can click the plus sign (+) next to the folder icon to display the subfolders. For Mac users, click the arrow next to the file folder to view subfolders. To create third- and fourth-level folders, repeat the same process, always beginning by highlighting the folder or subfolder in which you want to create the new folder.

Current Microsoft operating systems enable you to save up to 65,534 files and folders within a single folder, so you don't have to worry about not having the capacity to create multiple subfolder layers. I suggest not having more than six subfile layers within one file folder. When six layers become inadequate, consider moving one of your file folders up one layer or consolidating files.

> **note** Sometimes, software programs automatically create a separate folder intended for data associated with a specific software in your My Documents folder. This folder is usually given the software name. Often this folder is empty or contains templates. If this is the case, you can delete it from your structure. You don't have to save documents in those folders for those documents to open. The exception is with databases and CM software, which also create a separate folder within your My Documents folder. Usually the database file is saved under the My Documents folder and not under the system folder so that, when you back up, all your data is located under one folder. If you use programs such as ACT! or FileMaker Pro, you should keep the separate file folder created under My Documents.

FIGURE 4.8

In Microsoft Explorer, click the folder in the left pane view and you see its contents displayed in the right pane view. Click the + next to the folder to display that folder's subfolders within the left-pane view.

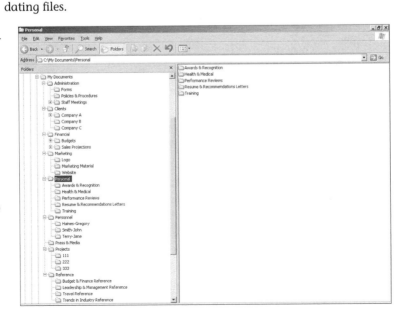

USING THE DETAIL VIEW IN MICROSOFT EXPLORER

Microsoft Explorer lets you choose from among a number of views that provide different information about your documents. To see the viewing options, click the Views icon in the Windows Explorer toolbar (typically, this is the last icon on the right; hover your mouse cursor over the icons to reveal their names). Though the list of available options varies depending on your version of Windows, all versions contain the Details option.

The Details view lists your file folders or document details, including the file type, the size, and the date it was created or modified. This is the best view to be in when organizing your documents because it displays more data about your files or documents. If you want to add other details in this view, go to your toolbar and select View, Choose Details (or Choose Columns for Windows 2000 and before); a separate Detail Settings window opens. You can click the box next to the detail or column you want to see in the Detail view. Click OK and that column of information is inserted into the Detail view. Unfortunately, the additional columns apply only to the file folder you have highlighted. However, you have to change the view for that folder only once because the settings remain in place the next time you open Microsoft Explorer.

You can also select the Detail view within the Open and Save As dialog boxes. Click the drop-down arrow next to the Views icon to select a view type.

To do list

- ☐ Consider which electronic files would benefit from standard naming conventions and implement those standards.
- ☐ Be consistent in naming your electronic documents.
- ☐ Consider adding the date to all your document names.

Developing Standard Naming Conventions

Choosing standard naming conventions for your filing system helps you name, file, and locate your electronic documents. Some categories of paper files always have a standard coding, such as personnel files that are labeled with last name, first name, and (possibly) employee ID number. Creating standard filenames for your electronic documents is similar to using standard filenames for your paper file folders.

Financial files and documents that are chronological in nature usually require standard naming conventions. If you have a folder called Budgets, for example, you might want to create subfolders by year. Coding the filenames and subfolders by year would be your standard naming convention for all documents to be stored in the Budgets folder. The data in the naming conventions is usually separated by spaces, dashes, or underscores, depending on your preference (see Figure 4.9).

To create standard naming conventions, consider the data that should always be entered in first, then the next set of data, and then the next. Sometimes in standard naming conventions for office-wide systems you leave the final part of the naming convention undesignated, so the user chooses that part of the name based on the document type.

FIGURE 4.9

In this filing structure, all budget documents are stored within the annual Budget folders contained within a Budgets subfolder of the Financial folder. The budget documents, shown in the right pane, use a standard naming convention.

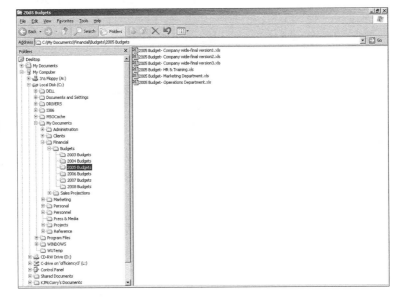

Even if you aren't applying standard naming conventions to a particular file folder, all your documents need appropriate filenames to make them easy to find and their data identifiable without opening the file. By default, electronic files are listed in most directories in numerical and alphabetical order. It is best to code your documents with the word you will think of first when you want to access it. Using spaces, dashes, and underscores between nouns and adjectives can help identify the document more quickly—as in **Company A-Bob Smith-sales letter-October 2000** versus **companyABobsalesltrOct2000**.

Avoid using vague descriptors such as *general* or *miscellaneous* in your filenames. These words usually are so vague that it makes recognizing the type of document harder in the future. Also avoid using only one word or descriptor in filenames; this makes it difficult to find documents in the future because of limited information in the filename.

Things You'll Need

- ☐ Second computer or second hard drive
- ☐ Removable media discs such as tape, CD-ROM, DVD, or Zip
- ☐ External or internal tape backup systems, such as tape, CD-ROM, DVD, Zip, or USB or Flash drives

Archiving Files

When you are reorganizing your hard drive, you are likely to find outdated documents. Some of these documents will clearly be of no value to you, and you can simply delete them. Some outdated documents, however, have value as historical reference; examples include past financial records, old business plans, completed projects, marketing materials, and correspondence. You might determine that all such documents become archivable after three years and therefore create a separate filing structure for historic documents to keep your current electronic filing system clean and uncluttered. It is much easier and cheaper to keep historical documents in electronic form.

caution Don't rename or move system file folders or documents within Windows or on the Mac, or those folders and documents within the Program Files folder on your computer. Most system files are created under Program Files or directly within the C drive or Mac drive. Changing the names or locations of these folders and documents can cause your software or hardware to malfunction.

You can create a folder labeled Historical or Archive in your My Documents or electronic file structure, or you can create one of those folders outside of your master outline structure. With either option, you can create a mirror image of your electronic file structure within this historical folder. As documents become outdated, you can move them into the same topical folder in the historical folder. Or you can set up subfiles in the historical folder by year and put outdated files or documents in it for the appropriate year. This is similar to archiving paper files in a file box and marking the year on the outside of the box.

If you have more than 5GB of archive data, you might consider having a separate computer or hard drive just for archive and historical information. Keeping your archived data on some sort of hard drive enables the data to automatically update as software and operating updates are made to your system.

Another option is to store historical and archive data on removable media such as a DVD, CD-ROM, tape, or Zip disk. Removable storage is effective if you have large client files full of pictures or graphic or video material that take up a large amount of space on your hard drive.

Be sure to always label your media with the date and type of documents included. You can write directly on the media or affix a label.

To do list

- ☐ Create shortcuts to your documents for quick viewing.
- ☐ Use the header and footer tool to insert the file pathname of your documents.
- ☐ Conduct a document search using the document name, date, or specific content.
- ☐ Print an index of your electronic file system for easy reference.

Finding Your Electronic Documents

Everyone wants the ability to get to her documents and information as quickly as possible. One of the challenges of electronic organization is to avoid wasting time finding documents or performing more than four or five clicks to find your document. Shortcuts provide one-click access to documents or folders. Most programs also enable you to set a new default file location, which also makes finding files faster and easier. And, if you simply can't remember where you've stored a file, you can use a file search to find the file based on its title, the date you last accessed the file, or even specific words or phrases in the file's content. Using shortcuts, changing file default locations, and performing effective searches can help you find your documents more quickly, more easily, and with less frustration and fewer mouse clicks.

Creating Shortcuts to Find Files Fast

To find your files quickly, create shortcuts to get to your file directory instantly, minimizing clicks. A *shortcut* is a type of file that acts like an Internet hyperlink to point to another file or document. A shortcut is not the original file nor a copy; if you double-click a shortcut, you open the original file or document. Shortcuts are usually placed on the desktop or in master folders to eliminate the need to drill down in a file structure to locate the original file or document.

note If you move the location of the original file or document, you need to re-create the shortcut. Deleting a shortcut does not delete the original file. Shortcut icons are identified by the small box containing an arrow that's always located in their bottom-left corners.

Adding Shortcuts to My Places or Shortcut Toolbar

Located on the left side of the Open or Save As window is a My Places toolbar (for PCs) or a Shortcut toolbar (for Macs). This is a quick way to open files and folders when you are in the Save As Window. PC users can add file folders to this toolbar by highlighting the folder in the window, clicking Tools in the window header, and clicking Add to "My Places", as shown in Figure 4.10. This automatically adds the file folder to the right column view. After it is in the column, right-click the folder to move it up or down in the list. Mac users can click and drag folders to the shortcut bar.

FIGURE 4.10

In this example, the Marketing folder is being added to the My Places toolbar on the left side of the Open dialog box.

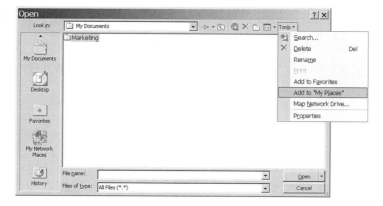

Creating File Shortcuts on the Desktop

With any file folder or document, you can create a shortcut on your desktop. This does not move the document to the desktop—it merely gives you one-click access to the document or folder from your desktop.

A quick way to add shortcuts to your desktop is by opening Windows Explorer or the Open or Save As window. Then highlight the folder or document, right-click, select Send To, and then select Desktop (see Figure 4.11). If you want to create a shortcut within a folder, open Windows Explorer, highlight the document, and select File, Create Shortcut.

> **caution** Be careful of creating too many shortcuts on your desktop. A desktop littered with too many shortcuts can become cluttered and difficult to use.

If you move the file or document to a different file location, you lose the link in your shortcut and have to re-create it. You can move a document or folder from a directory and onto the desktop by clicking and dragging it (using either PC or Mac).

Changing the Default File Location

The default file location is the drive and file that an application automatically points to when you use the Open or Save command. Usually, the default file location is set to your My Documents folder on your C drive under your user profile. If you use another drive or have created a folder other than My Documents for your electronic files, you should set your default file location to point to that location.

Mac users can open each Microsoft Office program and select File, Preferences, File Locations. Highlight Documents and click the Modify button to select a destination. Each Microsoft program for PCs has its own way to accomplish this task. In Word select Tools, Options to open the Options dialog box. Click the File Locations tab, highlight **Documents**, and click the Modify button (see Figure 4.12). Select the folder or drive you want to use as a default location for storing documents in Word; then click OK to close all the windows.

FIGURE 4.11

In Windows Explorer, you can create shortcuts of files or documents directly on your desktop. Highlight the file or document; right-click; and select Send to, Desktop.

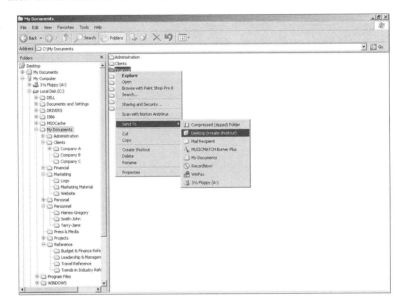

FIGURE 4.12

In Microsoft Word, you can change the default file location under the General tab of the Options dialog box. Highlight **Documents** and click the Modify button to find the drive and file you want Word to automatically open and save to.

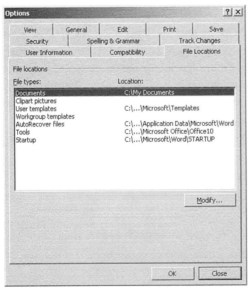

Inserting the Filename and Pathname on Document Pages

If you are printing documents for viewing, you can use the header and footer tool to insert the filename and pathname on each printed page, so you and others can know where the document is stored within your system. The few extra seconds required to use this tool can save you and others significant time when locating the file in the future. Here are instructions for using the Header/Footer tool in Word and Excel:

- In Microsoft Word, select View, Header and Footer; then select Header or Footer Location. In the Header and Footer toolbar, click the Insert Auto Text button and then click File Name and Path. The full file path is automatically inserted into the header or footer.

- In Microsoft Excel, select File, Page Setup; then click the Header and Footer tab. Click either Custom Header or Custom Footer. You then see an icon that is a file folder, and if you click that icon, it automatically inserts the file path. In either Microsoft application, the file path changes automatically if you rename the file or put it in another folder.

To do list

- ☐ Develop a schedule for purging your electronic file system of out-of-date or otherwise unnecessary files.
- ☐ Create a temporary file folder in your electronic system for documents or downloads that have only temporary value.
- ☐ Delete and purge old and outdated documents.

Conducting a Document Search

When looking for documents, you can use the Find or Search function to automatically search a specific file or drive to find documents. You can search for files based on the filename, the date the file was created or modified, or specific text contained within the file. In most programs, you activate the Search function by clicking a Search button or choosing a Search option from the main menu. In Windows Explorer, for example, click the Search button in the main toolbar, as shown in Figure 4.13. In the Open window of any Microsoft program, click the Tools button, and then select Search.

With all these search options, the Search window automatically opens. Complete the fields in the Search window to do an automatic find for the file or document you are looking for.

In the Search window in Windows Explorer, you can click the arrow next to More Advanced Options to search subfolders and system folders.

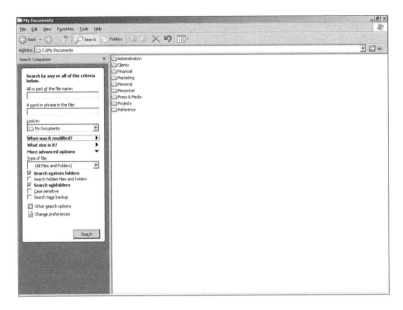

Keeping the Good Stuff Versus the Old Stuff

On a consistent basis your hard drive collects a number of outdated and unnecessary files. It is important to purge your electronic files periodically to keep your system in order, make necessary files easier to locate, and free up system storage space.

Here are some suggestions of documents and or files you can delete:

- Documents that are unnecessary or outdated
- Documents that are associated with old programs you no longer use or can access
- Temporary files and documents
- Empty file folders

Deleting Files and Folders

Ideally, when you run across unnecessary documents as you use your file structure, you should take the time to delete them on the spot. This periodic maintenance is a huge time-saver for two reasons: It makes your annual file purging faster and easier, and it reduces the number of files you have to scroll through to find the document you want.

You can delete files in PCs or Macs through Windows Explorer, through the Mac Drive, or in the Open and Save As window of Microsoft programs by highlighting the file and then pressing the Delete key, clicking the Delete icon, or selecting Delete from the context or File menu. Alternatively, you can drag the file to the Recycle Bin.

Using the Recycle Bin or Trash Folder

When you delete files in PCs and Macs, they are not actually deleted entirely from your system. Deleted files in Windows for PCs are moved to a Recycle Bin folder; deleted files on the Mac are moved to a Trash folder. If you need to restore a deleted file, merely open the Recycle Bin or Trash folder, highlight the deleted file, and select Restore to restore the file to its original file folder. Or you can drag the deleted file onto the desktop; from there, you can move it to the appropriate file folder.

caution If you delete from external media such as CD-ROMs and Zip disks, the deletion is usually a permanent delete, as opposed to moving it to the Recycle Bin. Also, if you delete from the server or a network system, the delete is also a permanent delete. Thus, be sure you are deleting correctly in these two circumstances.

To empty the Recycle Bin, right-click the Recycle Bin icon and select Empty Recycle Bin; this deletes the files permanently. For Mac users, just click the Trash icon and hold—the Empty Trash option appears.

Purging Electronic File Systems

You should purge your electronic files at least annually to keep your filing system current and dependable. It is usually easiest to begin purging your document files by sorting them by date. In Windows Explorer, go to the Detail view and click the header labeled Modified. This automatically sorts your documents or folders in date order. If you want to sort your documents by the Created Date, you must change the preferences on that file folder to include the Created Date in the Detail View (View, Choose Details). Review the oldest files first and then review the more current ones. This is the easiest method to quickly search, purge, and delete outdated documents.

Then, scan through each file folder and subfolder and delete duplicate files and drafts you no longer need. Click the header Name to sort your files by alphabetical order again. If you find you can't distinguish between various versions of your documents, consider changing your naming conventions to add dates or version numbers to future documents. Good naming conventions help make periodic purges easy and fast.

Disk Cleanup third-party software can help with automatic cleanup and optimize your PC hard drive. These programs purge your system of unwanted file fragments, cookies, duplicate files and or folders, and other temporary and unnecessary files from Internet downloads and uninstall functions that slow down computer performance. Two recommended file system cleaning applications are System Cleaner (www.pointstone.com/products/systemcleaner/) and jv16 Power Tools (www.jv16.org).

Creating and Purging Temp Files

In addition to the system and hidden temp file directories you learned about in Chapter 3, you might want to create a temp directory to store files that can be deleted immediately after their use, or shortly thereafter. You might choose to store Internet downloads you do not need permanently as temp files, for example.

You can create a Temporary folder to provide a quick and easy place to store documents that are only for temporary use. You can periodically purge all contents of your Temporary folder, deleting anything you've already used and need no longer store. To name your temp folder, insert an underscore or a numerical number before the word *Temporary*, as in **_temp** or **1 Temporary**. That way, the folder is automatically placed at the top of your file structure for quick and easy access, as shown in Figure 4.14.

FIGURE 4.14

Here, is a sample of a temporary folder created in the sample electronic file structure.

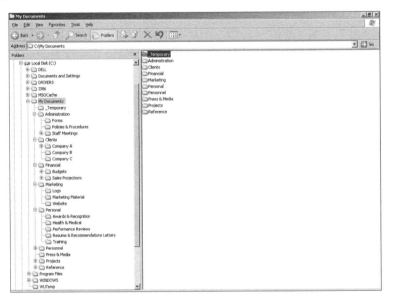

When you create a Microsoft document, the system automatically creates a temporary file of that document; this temp file is supposed to be automatically deleted when you save and close the document. However, if your system freezes or shuts down suddenly, the temp files aren't automatically deleted. After you've recovered the latest version of the document, you can delete these unnecessary temp files, which can be recognized by the tilde (~) in front of the filename and the **.tmp** file extension (you learn more about file extensions later in this chapter).

 Anytime you run Windows, some temp files are in use by the Windows operating system. If you try to delete these files, you get a message that the file cannot be deleted. It is recommended you ask your computer consultant before deleting those temporary files.

If you want to search for all the temporary files in your system or certain file folders, here is how you can do a one-step review. Open Windows Explorer and go to the Search function. In the field labeled Search for Files, type ***.tmp**, and then select the file folder or drive you want to search in the Look in field. This lists all the temporary files contained in that file folder or drive. Then highlight all those temporary documents you want to delete and press the Delete key. The files are moved to the Recycle Bin.

For Mac users, **.tmp** files are deleted automatically when you shut down your system.

Identifying File Types When Purging Files

When purging electronic documents, often you see files you can't identify by name or file extension. A *file extension* is the group of three or four letters that follow the period in all filenames. These file extensions tell your operating system which application or program the file was created in or relates to. With Macs, you do not see the file extension; the Mac automatically knows the associated software.

File extensions can also indicate whether a file is a document, system, or temporary file—information that can help you determine whether to delete the file during a system purge. The following list includes some file extensions and describes the types of files they indicate:

- **Microsoft Office files (.doc, .xls, .ppt, .mdb, .wps, .pst)**—Microsoft has standard filename extensions for its software applications. Word = **.doc**; Excel = **.xls**; PowerPoint = **.ppt**; Access = **.mdb**; Works = **.wps**; Outlook = **.pst**.

- **Temporary files (.tmp)**

- **System and application files (.exe, .dll, .ini)**—Most application and system files are in separate file folders stored on your hard drive and are not associated with data files. Most of these folders should be kept intact and not deleted, renamed, or moved from folders. If you created specific user functions for files or documents in Microsoft, you might see documents that have **.ini** extensions in your data files. These are configuration settings and should usually not be deleted. All **.exe** files are application files. The **.dll** files are typically extension files of a particular application.

- **Compressed files (.zip)**—Most compressed files are created with a **.zip** file extension, which programs such as WinZip and StuffIt produce.

note If you save an Internet page as an HTML file, the system often saves the pictures from that page, such as the logos and banner ads, in a separate file folder. If you delete this file folder of graphics, it usually deletes the separate HTML file itself. If you want the Internet page, go back to the website and try to save it in a printer-friendly format. In this form, it does not save the graphics in a separate folder. Or, you can save the file as an Adobe **.pdf** file that does save the entire page as one document.

- **Text-based files (.txt, .rtf)**—Usually filenames with a **.txt** and **.rtf** extension are text-based documents that can be opened in most standard word processing software across PC and Mac platforms.

- **Graphic, video, and picture files (.bmp, .tiff, .jpg, .mpeg, .gif, .png)**—Most graphic, video, and picture documents are quite large and take the most amount of file space on a computer system. Graphic file extensions can vary depending on which graphic software you are using.

- **Adobe documents (.pdf)**

- **Internet files (.html)**

For a complete list of file extension definitions, go to http://www.stack.com/file/extension/ or http://www.computerhope.com/dosext.htm#01.

To do list

- ☐ Create a paper filing system that parallels your master outline and electronic file structure.
- ☐ Use paper documents only temporarily and keep document archives electronically.
- ☐ Purge your paper files as you use them.
- ☐ File immediately and avoid "to file" piles.
- ☐ Consider scanning documents to save historic and archived documents electronically and reduce filing.

Managing Paper Files

Whether you want to become more paperless or not, the reality remains that there is still paper to manage in any office. The three organizing principles highlighted in Chapter 2, "Organizing Basics," apply to creating your paper system:

- **Consolidate**—Get rid of all the paper documents you no longer need and consolidate the same subject matter together.

- **Categorize**—Relate all your paper documents to some category or topic.

- **Create a home**—Determine which paper files will be kept where.

If you want to reduce your paper automatically, I suggest you first become more mindful of what you print! And when you've printed electronic documents to read away from your computer, remember to recycle those printouts when you've finished with them. That reduces the amount of space you'd consume filing those unnecessary hard copies and helps cut down on paper waste.

Things You'll Need

- ❑ Label maker
- ❑ Your master outline structure you created in Chapter 3
- ❑ Filing drawers/cabinets
- ❑ Filing supplies, including Manila folders, hanging files, labels, hanging tabs, and a pen

Creating a Filing System

When creating your paper filing system, refer to your master outline structure and be sure your paper filing system reflects that structure, as well as that of your electronic system. Nevertheless, the paper and electronic systems will have some differences. Some categories of files won't be necessary in your paper-based system, and some won't appear in your electronic structure. Keeping these differences in mind, however, try to keep the systems as similar as possible to make your stored information easier to locate, maintain, and access.

Categorizing and Locating Files and Folders

Determine which primary categories you need in your paper-based system and think about the best location for those categories. Ideally, the files you access most often should be closest to you in the office—you might store them, for example, in your desk's filing drawers. Categories you use less frequently could be in filing cabinets farther away from your desk.

Here are some typical examples of major categories that might be used in a paper filing system and suggested locations for those categories:

- **Active file drawer**—These are files that are the active projects, initiatives, and issues you are dealing with. It might also include quick reference information, such as upcoming travel, phone lists, and forms you use frequently. The active file drawer should be the drawer closest to you and the easiest to open. Most often it is either your right or left desk file drawer.

- **Reference file drawer**—These are files that are reference and topic-related information, such as articles and handouts. You might have these files in alphabetical order or grouped by subcategory—whichever you find easiest. These files should be within arm's reach or a chair's slide away. The type of drawer will depend on the amount of reference information you have.

- **Personal drawer**—These are files that are related to you and of a personal or personnel nature, such as awards, résumé, health and medical, training, travel, and other personnel documentation your company gives you. These files do not need to be near you unless you access them frequently. They can be located in a drawer farther away from your desk.

- **Confidential files**—These are files and documents that are confidential and private that you might want located in a separate, secure filing cabinet or drawer. Personnel records, financial information, or personal documents you do not want others to have access to could be located in a lockable drawer. If your drawers or cabinets do not have locks, you can purchase locks separately or consider purchasing a new locking file cabinet.

- **Business, projects, and clients drawer**—These are files that are related to the business of your company. This drawer (or drawers, depending on the number of files you keep) might contain files related to clients, projects, financial information, programs, or any other information you have created in your master outline. These files should be within arm's reach because you will probably need more frequent access to them.

Tabbing and Labeling

Ideally it is best to have a standard hanging file folder system. The hanging tabs for all major categories of documents should be placed in a straight line, centered in the hanging file. Be sure to place your tabs in the front of file. This enables you to add hanging folders and other folders behind the file, creating more room for the category (see Figure 4.15).

You can color-code tabs within your paper filing system, using a specific color for each primary category of files and subfiles. This coding makes identifying specific types of files within the file drawer easier. Avoid making each tab in one line a different color because that scheme can make it more difficult to visually identify an individual file or file type.

The third line in your outline, or subcategories of the second line, can be created as hanging tabs or file folders, or a combination of both. The third line hanging tabs are usually placed in a straight line and justified either to the far right or left. The idea is to create a visual in your filing cabinet of the master outline structure so that, when you open the file drawer, it is very easy to see your category line structure.

The major categories should be placed in the center line of the hanging folder. The subcategories should be placed either justified right or left in a straight line. When labeling your file folders, think about how you want to access the documents. If you want to see data chronologically, for example, then label file folders by annual date.

Label-making machines are easy to use, files labeled with label makers look better, and their names are easier to read. You are more apt to file documents quickly if you can see the file in three seconds or less. Label makers are a great investment for any office. Dymo (www. dymo.com) and Brother (www.brother.com) both make user-friendly and durable products. I prefer the desktop machines because of the portability. But the label makers that connect via USB port to your computer are also handy because you can print directly from your computer.

tip Code the file location directly on the document. You can write directly on the upper-right corner, use a sticky note, or highlight the title or keyword. Use a method that will be easy for you to do. Then, when you do go to file something, you'll easily remember the location. This is also helpful if you have an assistant who helps with filing.

FIGURE 4.15
The paper filing structure shown here uses the sample master outline.

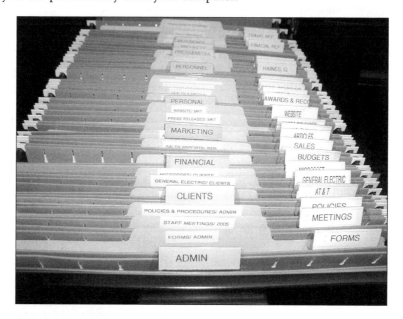

Keeping Your System Up-to-Date

Very few people like to tackle their to-file pile; usually, filing is the last action step on anyone's priority list. You can avoid this problem by filing papers immediately or at the end of each day. This becomes a doable daily action item and your information always is located where you can quickly get at it. The few minutes it takes for you to file daily will save hours of time in the future.

Along with daily filing, I suggest going through all your files annually to fix any filing errors and purge unnecessary documents that have slipped through the cracks during your regular purges. Purging annually keeps you connected with your system and information. An annual file cleanup keeps your entire filing system current and helps to guarantee that you will continue to use it. Also, during the course of the annual purge, you invariably will run across files you have forgotten about but that contain useful information.

Don't create new folders to avoid purging unnecessary documents from an existing folder. If you take this "shortcut," you end up with the same project in multiple files with your data scattered, fragmented, outdated, and difficult to access. When your files and documents stay current, you can trust your files and consistently use them.

Archiving Paper Files

As with electronic files, you might want to archive paper files. Again, these are files or documents you don't use on a regular basis but must keep for historical, legal, or tax purposes. Refer to the "Legislative Retention Compliance" section in Chapter 2 for more information on which types of files to archive.

Here are some options for archiving paper files:

- **Store them in a separate drawer**—You can designate one file drawer that will house all your historical paper files. This file drawer could be located in your private office (or cubicle) or in your office's general filing cabinets. As mentioned previously, private archived documents (personal financial information, personnel records, and so on) should be stored in a locked drawer or other secured location under your control.

- **Store them in a banker's box**—You can purchase and store your archive files in a separate banker's box or file storage boxes. Be sure to label the outside of the box with the contents and date of each box. Store the box in a closet, storage area, or offsite storage facility.

- **Scan and save them electronically**—You can also scan your historical documents and save them electronically and then dispose of the paper files (saving and archiving documents as necessary for tax records). The next section covers scanning in detail.

note America Recycles Day is a nonprofit organization that seeks to educate and encourage Americans to recycle. They hold an annual event on November 15, with local recycling initiatives taking place around the country. This could be an optimal time to schedule an annual information purge in your office. For more information, visit the website at www.americarecyclesday.org.

Scanning Paper Documents for Electronic Storage

To free up filing cabinet space, you might consider scanning documents in electronic form. This solution is useful for storing historical documents you no longer access, for storing articles or documents that are not in electronic form, or for collecting a series of paper documents into a single electronic document. Beyond creating more file space, scanning enables documentation to be readily accessible from your desk rather than in a filing cabinet, warehouse, or the basement storage.

tip If you have a lot of historical, financial, or legal documentation to scan and don't want to scan it yourself, scanning services can do that for you. Check your local directory for "document imaging" to find a service in your area.

Choosing Scanning Software and Equipment

Most full-sized office copy machines have scanning capabilities, as do small home office copiers. If you need to purchase a scanner and have documents that are longer than 25 pages, consider getting a scanner that has an automatic feed as opposed to a flatbed scanner.

tip Visit *PC World*'s website (www.pcworld.com). On their site, click Product Guides and click Scanners; this lists and reviews *PC World*'s top choices for scanners.

Most scanners/copiers/printers come with basic scanning software, which you can use to scan and save documents in that software's file type. Because scanning software can get outdated, you should save scanned documents in a common format, such as **.txt**, **.doc**, or **.pdf**. The most common scanning conversion format is in Adobe, or a **.pdf** file. The **.pdf** format is usually the recognized format for legal and tax documents because the document remains in its original format. The IRS and legal entities accept scanned documents "that display a high degree of integrity, legibility and credibilty."

Scanning software usually has optical character recognition (OCR) capabilities. OCR is the capability to read the document and convert it into text format so the data can be manipulated. Thus, you can scan in a document and save it in Word or a text-based format. This then gives you the capability to manipulate and use the text from the scanned document. Again, I do not suggest converting or saving in a text-based format for scanned legal and tax documents.

caution If you are unsure whether the type of documents you have will be accepted electronically for the IRS or legal purposes, please consult with your accountant and attorney.

A website called Scan Tips (www.scantips.com) offers more detailed information about scanning capabilities and how to scan effectively. It has some great suggestions on maximizing resolution, especially for photos. About.com also has some great tips on scanning; go to this direct link: http://desktoppub.about.com/od/scanning/.

Summary

In this chapter, you've learned how to organize and maintain both an electronic and paper filing system. Having a clear and consistent file structure for both electronic and paper-based information is important to good time management and work day organization. You also learned why it's important to take the time to purge both your paper and electronic files regularly. By doing this, you will be able to file and access your information much more easily. Information that is organized well is a powerful asset in your job.

Following are some of the major action steps suggested in this chapter:

- Create an electronic file structure that parallels your master outline structure.
- Name documents consistently. Use standard naming conventions when applicable.
- Create shortcuts on your system to go immediately to your file directory.
- Create a temporary file for temporary documents, and purge it periodically.
- Develop a paper file system that parallels your electronic system.
- Consider scanning in paper files that are not in electronic form.

In the next chapter, "Using Your Contact Software to Its Full Potential," we discuss how to track your contacts, calendar, and action list electronically. We also discuss how and why you should use personal digital assistants (PDAs) or handheld organizers.

Using Your Contact Software to Its Full Potential

5

Y ou can choose from among a wide range of software that can track information about contacts, sales, meetings, appointments, tasks, follow-ups, email, and other information and communications. In addition to contact and information management software, many people use handheld devices to track appointments, contact information, and so on. Depending on your job, your business, and your current computer system, you probably have at least some type of software system for tracking some or all of these items. In this chapter, you learn how to use these tools to make your workday more efficient and well-organized.

In this chapter, you learn about the various types of contact and personal information management software available today and how to best use these tools in your work day. This chapter also talks about handheld devices and their uses. The information you learn here will help you choose and begin using these time-management products. But if you feel you need more in-depth instruction, you might consider taking a class or buying a complete reference that discusses the specific products you choose and use.

To do list

☐ Learn the difference between contact management, personal information management, customer relationship, and database software.

☐ Learn the capabilities of each type of software.

Choosing Software to Manage Contacts and Schedules

Contact management (CM) or personal information management (PIM) software is your best choice for tracking personal day-to-day information. These are the programs I recommend to enhance or replace your current paper planner. CMs and PIMs perform many of the same functions, but PIMs are used to manage contact and schedule information that is available for viewing by one person only. CMs manage this data for groups of people, providing multiple-user access.

Microsoft Outlook, Best Software's ACT!, Novell's GroupWise, Palmsource's Palm OS, and IBM's Lotus Notes are some examples of popular CM and PIM software products.

CMs and PIMs are just some of the products you can use to track and coordinate your work day information. Database software is useful for gathering and organizing large collections of data, as are customer relationship management (CRM) programs. And nearly all businesses use email these days, so you probably have an email management program in use right now. Some email management programs coordinate with other scheduling and calendaring programs, as you learn in this section of the chapter.

Although entering your data into the software can take more time than setting up a paper planner, after you've entered your contact, client, and scheduling data, the CM or PIM software becomes an instant resource for locating information and tracking your contacts and schedule quickly and easily. Plus, the software enables you to view, organize, and report data in multiple ways. This saves time when you need to find an important contact number or information related to your next meeting.

Things You'll Need

☐ Business cards

☐ Contact management or personal information management software

☐ Sticky notes or other pieces of paper containing notes about tasks, appointments, and contact information

Contact Management Software

Contact management programs, such as ACT!, Goldmine, and Now Up-to-Date, track contact information such as names, addresses, and telephone numbers. These products enable multiple users to access the same contact information and database, and they provide separate task and calendar functions. Many of these programs also have an email component or interact with other leading email programs such as Microsoft Outlook. CM software is designed to center all data around a contact entry, and thus all tasks and calendar items are associated and linked with a contact. Almost all CM software syncs, or shares data, with handheld devices.

Personal Information Managers

Personal information managers, such as Entourage, GroupWise, Lotus Notes, Outlook, Palm, and Daylight, allow an individual user to record personal information such as appointments, contact information, tasks, and other miscellaneous types of information and lists. Most businesses also use these programs for email management because they have very good multiuser capabilities. Unlike CMs, PIMs do not allow users to interact with the same contact data. The data in a PIM is inaccessible to others unless specific permission is granted; with permission, others can view calendar details, tasks, and contact lists. PIMs also have limited linking functionality to tie calendar and task items to contact information.

Database Software

Database software, such as Access and FileMaker Pro, typically is designed to manage customer and client data. With database software, you have complete control of how you want to organize, collect, and view information. CM and PIM tools use software in which the database has been predeveloped and the basic code and functionality cannot be modified. Often companies develop Access or FileMaker Pro as a customized and smaller scale customer relationship management tool that can be shared company-wide. These database programs can be particularly useful in comparing, sorting, and reporting on specific fields of data that a CM or PIM might not be able to provide.

Database software enables the user to fully customize his own database. Database software isn't intended for tracking day-to-day personal time management data and communications information, such as tracking calendar, action lists, or email as with CMs or PIMs.

Customer Relationship Management

CRM software, such as Seibel, PeopleSoft, and SalesForce.com, typically offers large-scale programs designed for full life-cycle interaction with marketing customers. These products specifically track sales, marketing, and business support functions that relate to customers, clients, and prospects. This tracking capability also can be used to produce reports that help to monitor and forecast customer preferences and sales. CRMs are intended for multiuser, company-wide use, rather than personal time- and contact-management functions. Although CRMs are not intended to be email managers, they usually interact with a company's primary email manager. Company employees can track client communications through their CRM tool and then use CM or PIM software to track their own personal day-to-day data.

Email Software

Email software products, such as Eudora, Outlook Express, and AOL, are designed solely to manage email, but all email managers do have an address book function that enables you to store contact information. They usually do not offer a way to track tasks nor calendar appointments and therefore cannot be classified as full PIMs. Most email programs interact with most CM software. If you currently like your email program but would like additional functionality, purchase a contact manager that interacts with your email program. Before you purchase your contact manager, check the software details online to make sure it can interact with your email software.

Comparing Contact Management and Personal Information Management Software Functions

The following table offers a comparison of functions available with the leading contact management and personal information management software. All products listed in this table offer contact information/address book features, as well as calendaring and action/task list tools. All the programs listed here also enable you to track notes and maintain an activity history. Other capabilities vary, as shown. Use the web address information to find more details about these products.

To do list

- [ ] Enter all business cards into your CM or PIM tool.
- [ ] Categorize and group all your contacts.
- [ ] Begin the habit of tracking notes for your contacts.

Software	Website	PC or Mac	Email Capabilities	Sync with PDAs	Customize Fields and Add Fields	Create Reports	Categorization and Grouping	Track Sales and Marketing	Attach Files to Records
ACT!	www.act.com	PC	Yes	Yes	Yes	Yes	Yes	Yes	Yes
Daylite	www.marketcircle.com	Mac	No	Yes	Yes	Yes	Yes	Yes	Yes
Entourage	www.microsoft.com	Mac	Yes	Yes	No	No	Yes	No	Yes
Goldmine	www.goldmine.com	PC	Yes	Yes	Yes	Yes	Yes	Yes	Yes
GroupWise	www.novell.com	PC	Yes	Yes	Yes	No	Yes	No	No
Lotus Notes	www.lotus.com	PC	Yes	Yes	No	No	Yes	No	No
Now Up-to-Date	www.nowsoftware.com	PC and Mac	No	Yes	Yes	Yes	Yes	No	Yes
Outlook	www.microsoft.com	PC	Yes	Yes	No	No	Yes	No	Yes
Palm Desktop	www.palmone.com	PC and Mac	No	Yes	No	No	Yes	No	No

Using Contact Management Software: Throw Away the Business Cards!

All CMs and PIMs have a location to track contact information. A given individual today might have four or more phone numbers; two to three email addresses; as well as separate mailing addresses for home, work, and one or more satellite offices. It can be difficult to track all this data on a business card or within a paper address book. The electronic tools discussed in this chapter give you multiple options for tracking all sorts of contact information related to an individual.

These tools offer a number of benefits over collecting and filing business cards. Often when we receive business cards, they end up scattered in a desk drawer or consolidated into a big stack. When we need that data, it is difficult to access or use. Relationships are a powerful tool in today's business world. Utilizing your contacts as resources and potential sales maximizes your business potential. After you enter business and contact information into a software tool, you have the power to market and utilize these contacts fully through mailings and email.

Entering Contact Data

All CMs and PIMs have standard fields for entering most basic contact and address information. Usually, there are fields for both home and office addresses and the option to enter three to four phone numbers and email addresses. After you enter an email or website address, the software creates a hyperlink for that address; when you click it, the link opens a new email message window or your default Internet browser.

> **caution**
>
> Always enter the correct information in the designated field. You might be tempted to enter an email address in the mailing address field simply because you only use the email address and want it to be immediately visible when you open the contact. But don't give in to that temptation! Keeping information stored in the appropriate fields maintains the integrity of your data when you sync with handhelds or need to import or export it into other software.

INSERTING OUTLOOK CONTACT INFORMATION INTO WORD

After you enter contacts and address information into the Contact file in Outlook, you can insert that data automatically in Word by adding the Outlook Address Book icon to the toolbar. This is a time-saver if you are creating mailing labels or customized letters and don't want to retype contact information. Here's how:

1. In Word, select View, Toolbars, Customize; the Customize window opens.

2. Click the Commands tab. In the Categories list, select Insert. Scroll down the Commands list until you locate the icon for the Address Book, as shown in Figure 5.1.

3. Click and drag the Address Book icon to the standard toolbar.

4. To insert an address in a Word document, click the Address Book icon; it automatically opens the Select Name window.

5. Select the names you want inserted and click OK. The addresses are inserted where your cursor is placed.

FIGURE 5.1

In the Customize window in Microsoft Word, you can add the Address Book icon to the standard toolbar and use it to insert address information from Outlook into any Word document.

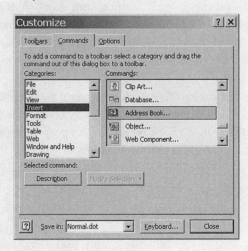

Categorizing or Grouping Contacts

Most CMs and PIMs have the capability to group or categorize contacts. This can be useful for multiple reasons, including sending group emails, creating mailing labels, printing phone lists, and tracking resources. The groups or categories you create might be similar to the primary categories you created in your master outline in Chapter 3, "Joining the Electronic Age of Organizing." Commonly used categories for grouping contacts include personal, vendors, clients or customers, prospects, association or organization names, types of industry, mailing lists, and project names.

Each software uses a different method for assigning a category or group to a contact. Most software includes in the contact window a field or tab used to assign categories or groups. If you click in this field or tab, you can assign specific groups and categories for each contact. Please refer to the Help menu to learn how to assign categories in your particular software.

To assign a category to an Outlook contact, follow these directions:

1. Open a contact window.

2. In the lower-left corner, click the Categories tab.

3. To enter a category names, click the Master Category List tab. This opens the separate Master Category List window.

4. Type the name of the category in the New Category field; then click Add. You can add multiple category names in this window.

5. Click OK to close the Master Category List window, and then click OK again to close the Categories window.

Most of the contacts you develop over time will have multiple relationships to you. For example, you might meet someone who is a potential client, then a friend, then a member of the same organization, and then a resource that you refer to other clients. Thus, you might need to classify a contact in more than one category or group. Most CMs and PIMs have the capability to assign a contact within multiple groups.

Most software provides various options for viewing contacts, listed by each category and group you have assigned. In Outlook, click the Contacts file folder. Then click View in the toolbar and select Current View. Select By Category to see a list of all your contacts grouped by the categories you have assigned.

If your CM or PIM allows, you might also consider creating subgroups. This is useful if your contacts relate to subgroups within a primary group.

If your CM or PIM does not have the capability to do subgroups, you can create subgroups by applying a naming convention. If you want to group your clients in subgroups by potential clients, former clients, active clients, and so on, as shown in Figure 5.2. Using this format keeps the group and subgroups in alphabetical order so you can see clearly which type of subgroups you have developed.

FIGURE 5.2
In Microsoft Outlook, you can create subcategories using a naming convention. An example of naming categories is shown here in the Categories window.

Taking Notes and Tracking History

All CMs and PIMs have the capability to track notes that relate to a particular contact. This function can be extremely useful for collecting and tracking information about a person and an organization. You can add data in the notes area as a means of remembering your last contact with someone or to record key information that you need to remember for your next contact. Because the notes are linked to specific contacts, the data they carry is always easy to find. Some CM/PIM software, including ACT!, Outlook, and GroupWise, has the capability to track notes separately and organize the notes by date and time. Other CM/PIM software, such as Entourage and Lotus Notes, has a blank text space available in which you can create your own standardized tracking method.

tip

Always put the date before any note entry so you remember when you wrote it. This date will also help you keep your contact information current by making it easier to delete outdated notes.

With Microsoft Outlook, there are two ways you can track notes for contacts: You can record information in the text space provided on the General tab, or you can create a new journal entry on the Activities tab. Tracking notes on the General tab typically makes the information easiest to view, especially if you have limited notes to take for each contact. Also, the notes field on the General tab is usually synced with your handheld. If you have a lot of information to record for a particular contact, creating a separate journal entry might be an easier way to organize and track your notes. A journal entry's notes, however, will not be synced with your handheld.

To create a new journal entry, follow these steps:

1. Highlight a specific contact.

2. Click Actions in the toolbar and select New Journal Entry for Contact.

3. In the New Journal Entry window, enter the topic or name of person in the subject line (see Figure 5.3).

4. Click the Entry Type drop-down list and select which type of note you would like to create.

5. Outlook automatically inserts the current date and time. You can change the date and time if you wish.

6. Write notes about a call or meeting in the text space provided.

7. When finished, click Save and Close. The journal entry is listed under the Activities tab. Double-click the journal entry to open the window and view the notes.

tip   *Time Saver*

When you receive a business card from a trade show, a networking event, or any other business or personal function, write on the back of the business card useful information about the contact that you learned. This information might include the date, event, and person who introduced you, alternative phone numbers or email addresses, hobbies and interests, and specific products or action items you discussed with this contact. When you get back to your home, office, or hotel, enter the notes into your CM or PIM tool.

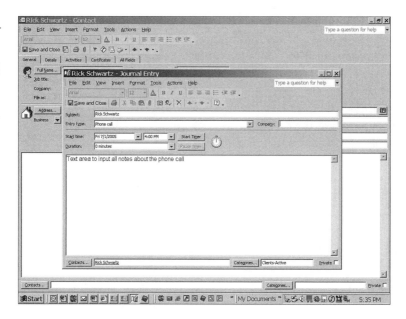

FIGURE 5.3
In Microsoft Outlook, you can create a new journal entry for a contact to track specific notes about a meeting or phone call.

To do list

- [ ] If possible, keep only one personal calendar for business and personal scheduling.
- [ ] Consider coding different types of meetings and events.
- [ ] Track all information related to a calendar item in the notes field.

Calendaring Efficiently

Using your CM or PIM as your primary calendar can be an efficient way to track your appointments and meetings. Calendar entries are easy to move when schedules change, even those for recurring meetings. If you have a CM tool, your calendar entries are automatically linked to a specific contact and you can track all upcoming and past appointments related to a specific person. You also have the ability to quickly track past year data without thumbing through old paper planners.

Unlike paper planners, electronic calendars let you enter data once and then organize it in multiple views. You can enter your appointments once, for example, and then view them by the day, week, or month. Multiple calendar views provide you with a more versatile planning tool. For example, if you are planning upcoming travel, seeing a month view initially is optimal. After you determine a good month and week, you might need to see a day view to show those items that need to be rescheduled.

MAINTAINING MULTIPLE SCHEDULES

Although most CMs and PIMs provide the functionality to set up separate calendars, I suggest that you maintain one calendar for business and personal items. Tracking all your meetings and appointments on a single calendar is the easiest and simplest method for maintaining your schedule. This approach avoids the potential for double-scheduling, and it makes viewing and organizing your daily, weekly, and monthly schedule simpler and more efficient.

If you have a lot of personal *and* professional appointments and meetings to track, you might need to use multiple calendars. If your calendar becomes too overloaded with data, the information can be difficult to read in one calendar view. If this is the case, you can create two separate electronic calendars (which most PIMs will allow) or reserve your electronic calendar for business and keep a paper-based calendar for personal appointments.

If you are a project manager with a large project, you might want to keep a separate calendar to track milestones and due dates. This is especially useful if you need to see one master view of a project. I suggest with project appointments and meetings that you also track them in your primary calendar. Having a separate project calendar, free of personal data, can be useful for sharing with others on the project. If you would rather see your project in one calendar view, use the option of assigning a color or category to all project meetings.

Entering Events

Creating a new calendar entry is easy within most CMs and PIMs. Typically, you double-click a time in the calendar view to open a blank calendar window. Or, you can click the button or icon that allows you to schedule an appointment or meeting to open the same new calendar entry window. In either case, you type the new information in the designated text boxes and then close the dialog box or window to add the entry to your calendar.

caution

Don't assign too many colors and categories to calendar entries. If your calendar view becomes busy with too many colors, that defeats the purpose of using these visual cues to quickly distinguish entry types. Ideally, try not to have more than six colors.

All CMs and PIMs have standard calendar fields and functions of subject, date, time, notes, reminders, reoccurrence, color-coding, and categorizing. You can develop your own guidelines for using these fields and functions to match your working style and the type of appointments you have. Using a consistent format for your calendar entries can make using your calendar more efficient. You can use the subject-line format, color-coding, and categories to quickly distinguish between different types of appointments (see Figure 5.4). You'll be able to determine which kinds of appointments make up your days, weeks, and months at a glance—making planning and scheduling easier and more efficient.

FIGURE 5.4
In this example, calendar appointments are coded by both color and naming convention.

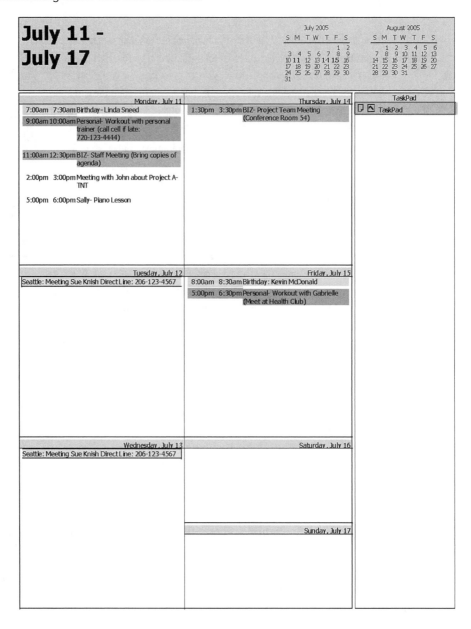

Most software enables you to schedule reoccurring appointments automatically. This reoccurring feature is usually located as a separate function within the appointment window as an icon or a tab. Setting reoccurrence for meetings saves time and the hassle of constantly reentering meetings that occur every day, week, or month.

Reminders or alarms can be set that sound an alarm and open a pop-up window at a designated time before a meeting or an appointment. The reminder function can be useful if you have a tendency to be late for appointments and need a reminder beforehand. Avoid setting reminders for every appointment, however; you will have a tendency to disregard them if they pop up too frequently. For the alarm function to operate, the software application usually must be open.

Adding Notes to Your Calendar

In the appointment window of most PIMs and CMs, you can use a note or comment field to record additional important information and details about a meeting or an appointment. These details usually get lost on the original invitation, on sticky notes, in emails, or in your paper notes. Tracking appointment details in the notes or comment field allows you to have all the data you need in one location, as shown in Figure 5.5. The notes and comment fields usually sync with most handheld devices, which is useful when you are not in your office and need to have those details right away.

tip Make a habit of confirming appointments a week or a few days in advance either by phone or email. When you confirm, clarify the time, date, and meeting location. Be sure to give the people you're to meet with the best way to contact you either by email or phone in case of cancellation or delay. When scheduling appointments, ask the other person to write down your phone number or directions—this gently encourages others to write the appointment on their calendar.

FIGURE 5.5

In the New Appointment window in Microsoft Outlook, you can record a wealth of important information about scheduled meetings, appointments, and events.

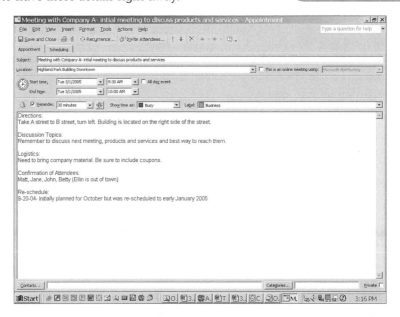

If you receive appointment details through email, you can copy and paste the data from the email into the notes and comment fields of your electronic calendar.

To create an appointment from an email in Microsoft Outlook, you simply click and drag an email into the calendar folder and it automatically copies the data into the appointment window. Then, you merely change the subject, the date, the time, and any other fields in accordance with the meeting details.

Keeping a Group Calendar

Most CMs and PIMs provide the capability to have an organization-wide calendar that is viewable by multiple people. A group calendar can be useful for tracking projects and activities for a group of people within a company, a department, an organization, or a project team. Depending on the group, you can track items such as employee leave, external and internal events, group meetings, and common deadline date activities.

To make group calendars more effective, I recommend you establish guidelines for entries. Make sure everyone follows standard coding, subject naming, or categorizing conventions, so that anyone within the group can always find and track appointments, meetings, events, and absences for all group members. The conventions you use are less important than ensuring that everyone within the group follows the same set of conventions so the calendar remains readable and useful for everyone.

Many people find it cumbersome to enter calendar items in both their personal and group electronic calendars. To avoid duplication, you can create the calendar entry in one calendar, copy that entry, and paste it into the other calendar. If the copy and paste function is unavailable between personal and group calendars, you can transfer calendar items via email.

To have easy access to the group calendar, consider creating a shortcut or bookmark on your toolbar. With many new versions of CMs and PIMs, such as with Outlook 2003, you can view multiple calendars side-by-side, which can make planning and scheduling much easier.

To do list

- ☐ Choose a method for tracking all action items.
- ☐ Create deadlines for all action items, and prioritize the items on your action list.
- ☐ Use the notes field to track information about action items.

Creating an Action List

An important part of time management is tracking all the many things you need to do and take action on in any given day. Most people refer to these tasks as *action items* or *to dos*. Depending on your job and the type of tasks you have, you can use any number of methods to track your action items. CMs and PIMs typically have separate Task or To Do windows in which to track your action items. In most CM and PIM software, scheduled tasks appear automatically in the Calendar view, either at the beginning of the day or in a separate task list located beside the calendar.

note Optimally, maintaining one master task list makes tracking all your action items and determining priorities easier. Many people choose to keep separate task lists for separate kinds of action items, such as personal, business, or project-specific actions. Most PIM/CM software enables you to create and track multiple task lists. If your software doesn't provide this capability, however, you can use Excel worksheets or other electronic means for tracking action items and to do lists.

To create an electronic task in your CM or PIM, click in the window or file folder marked Task or To-Do and use the tools and options available within the Task or To Do window (each software uses its own procedure for creating a new task or to-do).

To create a new task in Outlook, click the Tasks folder. In the toolbar, click the icon of a clipboard with a check mark to open a new task window. You can also select File, New, Task from the upper toolbar. Once in the new task window, complete the field information, as shown in Figure 5.6.

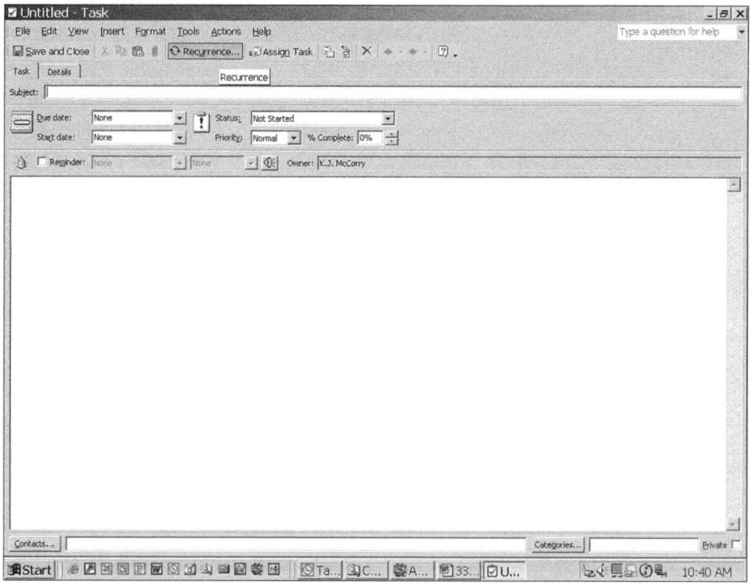

FIGURE 5.6

Use the Task tab window in Outlook to create a new task. If you click the Recurrence icon in the toolbar, you can schedule tasks to reoccur on a daily, weekly, monthly, or yearly basis.

Categorizing Tasks Within Your Action List

Most CMs and PIMs have the capability to sort, view, and organize all tasks by categories or groups in one master task list. If your action list is lengthy, you might need to use categories to separate tasks associated with personal items, business items, projects, external organizations and associations, or volunteer work. Some CMs or PIMs enable you to create separate task lists for different projects within the software. Here are some common task categories:

- **Daily tasks**—Varied action items that must be completed by a specific date or time. These tasks are usually ones you have promised to complete by a particular date some time in the future. You might meet with a client, for example, and they request a proposal be sent to them by their next staff meeting the following month. This task does not need to be done today, or even this week, but it's vital that it be completed on time. Such tasks are easily forgotten and therefore need to be tracked. Daily tasks are best tracked either through the task window in your CM or PIM software, where a date can be assigned for each task. When that assigned date arrives, it is up to you to determine to complete that task that day or reassign it to a future date, if you need more time.

- **Routine tasks**—Done on a daily, weekly, or monthly basis, such as sorting mail, data entry, ordering, performing maintenance tasks, paying bills, sending invoices, or running errands. Most individuals know they need to check their email and snail mail daily and don't necessarily need to track these routine items. But weekly or monthly routine tasks are easy to overlook and might need to be tracked on an action list. With most CMs and PIMs, you can schedule reoccurring tasks so that they always appear on your calendar or task list at designated intervals. The reoccurrence feature is usually found under the task window in CMs and PIMs as a toolbar icon, tab, or check box.

> **tip** Most routine tasks are imposed responsibilities and can take up an enormous amount of time. If you find that your day is being spent only doing routine tasks, you might want to consolidate the tasks in one limited time period on a weekly or daily view. For example, the mail comes daily but you might not need to sort and deal with it on a daily basis. Thus, designate an area to collect daily mail and then deal with it on a weekly basis. Think of all your routine tasks and how you can consolidate them into one period of time to save time.

- **Immediate tasks**—Need to be done right away and can be completed in just a few minutes. Tasks such as returning phone calls, scanning newsletters, signing documents, answering quick questions, and filing don't need to be tracked if they are done immediately. If you can't respond immediately to such a task, however, you should enter it as an action item in your electronic task list (or paper planner) so you don't forget to take care of it. That way, you can return to the task at hand and not worry about remembering a task that remains to be done.

Scheduling Projects

Projects are large initiatives that require multiple action steps and happen over an extended period of time. If you're managing multiple projects, you can keep separate project action lists so you can see in one view what needs to be accomplished with each project. Create categories or groups for each project, as shown in Figure 5.7.

note If you find that your work life involves constantly dealing with unscheduled tasks such as urgencies and crises, it might be because of poor planning or lack of planning. Did you create the crisis yourself because you failed to take action ahead of time? If the answer is "yes," you might need to become more diligent in tracking your tasks, assigning due dates, and reviewing your task list daily. Although some last-minute emergencies are unavoidable, crisis management shouldn't be the normal work mode for most jobs.

FIGURE 5.7
In Microsoft Outlook, you can create a new category for each project. Click the Categories tab located in the lower-right corner of the task window. To assign a category to a task, click in the box next to the category and then click OK.

You can sort and view tasks by category to create a separate project list view, as shown in Figure 5.8. Using categories enables you to track all projects and their action items in one master list, while also being able to track and view by each category or group.

If you want to maintain a separate project list, you have a few options for doing so. You can create a new task folder in your CM or PIM or track projects separately in a Word or Excel document. You also can use project-management software, which we will discuss in Chapter 8, "Managing Projects Effectively." Remember, however, that when you maintain separate task and action lists, coordinating all your project activities becomes more difficult.

FIGURE 5.8

In Microsoft
Outlook, you can see
all your tasks in the
simple list view. To
see tasks by
assigned category,
select View, Current
View, By Category.

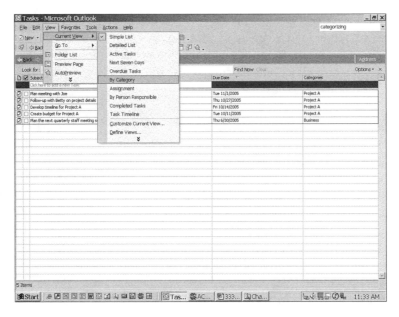

Initiatives and Development

These type of tasks are usually large goals and initiatives that require time and thought, such as creating new manuals, writing new procedures and policies, investigating and reporting, doing research, developing business ideas and strategic initiatives, and so on. Initiatives and development tasks typically are considered highly important yet do not have deadline dates associated with them. Many people don't track these tasks, making it easier to procrastinate and delay their completion.

I suggest breaking these types of tasks down into smaller, more doable action steps. This makes tracking them and integrating them into your day or week easier. You might want to keep a separate list of the larger goals or initiatives; when you have identified the smaller action steps to accomplish those goals, you can use your electronic task list to track them.

Reading and Review

In the Information Age, it is highly valuable to keep up on current trends and your industry. Many people feel unproductive, however, if they read during the work day. If reading external or internal information such as journals, books, reports, newsletters, Internet articles, and so on is an important part of your responsibilities, you should schedule reading and review time as an action item on your action list. Be sure to keep the material you need to read in a designated location, so you can quickly find those items when it comes time to read.

Prioritizing Action Items

Many time-management gurus have emphasized the importance of prioritizing each and every task to ensure that all your tasks are accomplished on time. Every task has its own place in the hierarchy of your daily responsibilities, depending on whether it needs to be done immediately or can wait until later. You can develop a coding method to indicate a task's priority level and establish due dates for all tasks to help plan your day and focus on meeting your priorities.

Creating Deadlines and Due Dates

You should assign a deadline or due date to all action items. Some action items come to you with deadline dates already predetermined, and other action items have no dates. Busy people have a tendency to focus on action items that have assigned due dates. Open-ended tasks are easier to postpone or forget entirely. I encourage you to assign a due date to every task you have for yourself or that you have delegated to others.

No amount of prioritizing will make an overly busy schedule doable. If you find that you have scheduled more than 10–15 tasks in one day, you might need to reassign certain tasks to future dates. As discussed in Chapter 1, "Knowing What You Want from Your Work Day," most due dates are negotiable. As soon as you see that your schedule is becoming unworkable, take action to negotiate deadlines to make your schedule more realistic. Waiting until the last minute to let others know you can't complete a task on time often breeds resentment, anger, and distrust. Failing to meet commitments also leads to poor planning and creates a stressful situation, so monitor and manage your schedule and time carefully to avoid such problems.

Assigning Priorities

Assigning priorities to tasks can help you plan your daily or weekly schedule around essential tasks. Most electronic task lists enable users to assign a high, medium, or low priority to tasks. You also can use the color-coding options to determine priority levels—for example, using red to mark high-priority tasks, blue to mark medium-priorities, and green for the lowest-priority tasks.

MAINTAINING YOUR FOCUS

The Franklin-Covey principle of time management determines tasks either as urgent or important. According to the Franklin-Covey principle, urgent action items are those received from outside influences and are not related to accomplishing overall mission and goals. The important action items are those determined by values, vision, and company goals. Important actions are part of your role and responsibility and help move important initiatives forward. The urgent action items, however, seem to be the tasks we spend most of our day accomplishing, while the important ones get pushed aside. In Stephen Covey's book *The Seven Habits of Highly Effective People*, he suggests switching that paradigm and focusing on your important tasks first before you deal with the urgent tasks. Always assign the important tasks as top priority. Doing this not only allows those important tasks to work their way into your work day first, but also focuses your time on what matters most and what you most want to accomplish. Usually, when you shift this paradigm, you feel like you are accomplishing more and being more productive.

If you have trouble determining the priority level of a given task, use the following checklist; the more of these items that apply to your task, the higher its priority:

- The task will significantly help the mission of the company or organization.
- The task is part of a major initiative or plan that, if accomplished, will solve a significant problem or improve operations.
- The task has a firm deadline date within the week.
- The task will create revenue or minimize expenses.

Tackling Your Action List

Although creating an action List and tracking action items enables you to plan and organize your day, it doesn't ensure that the action items will get done. At the beginning of each day, you should review your task list and focus on those items you have scheduled for that day.

Upon completion of a task, you have the option in most CMs and PIMs to delete the task or mark it as completed. Deleting tasks erases all record of the task. If you want to keep a record of your completed tasks, mark the task completed; then the electronic task is archived in your system.

Keeping Task Notes

Most task windows contain fields marked either Notes, Comments, or Details, in which you can insert additional information about a task. Keeping task notes is a useful way to collect all information about a task in one view, as shown in Figure 5.9.

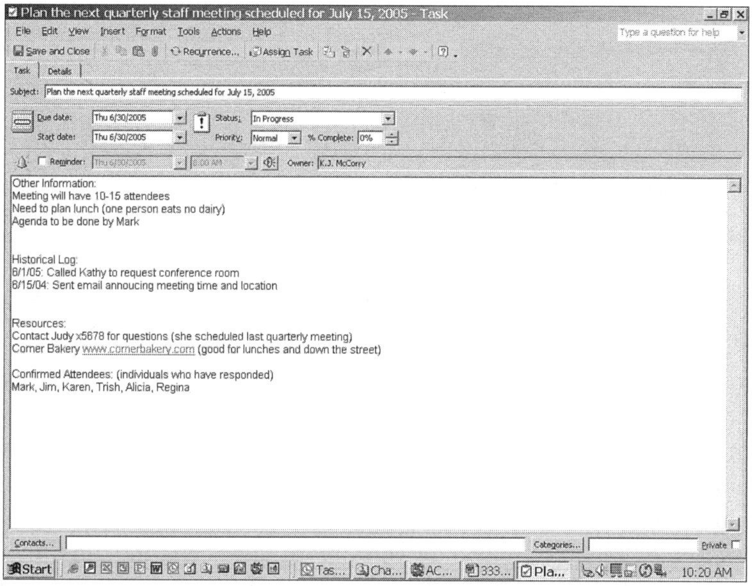

FIGURE 5.9

These tracking notes have been recorded within a task window in Microsoft Outlook.

WHAT SHOULD YOU STOP DOING?

Jim Collins wrote the best-selling book *Good To Great*, about practices and policies that make good companies even better. In his book, he discusses the concept of the "stop doing" list. He explains, "Most of us lead busy but undisciplined lives. We have ever-expanding 'to do' lists. Trying to build momentum by doing, doing, doing—and doing more. It rarely works. Those who built the good to great companies, however, made as much use of the 'stop doing' lists as 'to do' lists."

There can always be an endless to-do list. Before tracking an action item, ask yourself whether it's really an important or necessary action to take. Is it going to significantly offer results? Is it going to cost more time and money than it's worth? If so, consider skipping the action altogether. If certain tasks were agreed upon by a group or your boss, talk it over with them first. Most project teams, staff, colleagues, and supervisors don't want to waste your time.

Also consider these same questions if you are going to delegate a task. Don't delegate an action item just because you want it off your list. Be certain the task is truly worth someone's time before you delegate it. Then, make sure you give it to the appropriate person. If not, you are just creating more unnecessary work for your colleagues.

To do list

☐ Learn about the most common types of handheld devices and their uses.
☐ Consider device options when choosing a handheld.

Taking the Data with You—Using Handhelds

Handheld devices, or personal digital assistants (PDAs), are another valuable tool for organizing your calendar, schedule, and contacts. PDAs are small, portable, handheld electronic devices that use computer technology to perform specific time management tasks, such as calendaring, maintaining contact lists, tracking tasks, organizing notes, sending or receiving email, serving as a telephone, and more. Most handheld devices are designed to sync with CM and PIM software on your desktop or laptop computer, so your information remains current and accurate on both your mobile and desktop organizing systems. If you do not have CM or PIM software, most handhelds come with standard PIM software, such as the Palm Desktop.

PDAs are convenient and portable tools for referencing and organizing your key information while not in the office. PDAs were designed to replace the paper planner and can be much more efficient in tracking day-to-day information.

Here are just some of the ways you can use a handheld device to make your work day more efficient and organized:

- Carry important contact, calendar, and task information with you and access it quickly.
- Use your handheld reference tools and third-party sotware as a portable reference source.
- Use your handheld device to access the Internet and manage phone and email contacts.
- Use your handheld to store and access documents.

Choosing a Handheld Device

The key to choosing a handheld device is determining what type of data you want with you and instantly available. Then you can purchase a handheld designed to provide simple access to that data. If you want to use your CM or PIM more and would like a handheld, I suggest starting with a basic, inexpensive model. If you have been using your CM or PIM tool for a few years and would like some

additional functionality, you might want to consider a handheld with more functionality.

Palm OS and Pocket PC Operating Systems

The most common operating systems used in handheld devices are the Palm OS and Windows Pocket PC systems. The Palm OS systems usually tend to be less expensive and offer limited memory and functionality. With the newer Palm models, the differences between OS and Pocket PC have been reduced. Palm OS models also operate with PCs or Mac computers.

Pocket PC systems run software that is similar to a mini Microsoft platform. Running these systems therefore typically requires more memory. Pocket PC handhelds also are usually more expensive because of the larger memory capacity. One of the advantages to Pocket PC systems is their capability to open Microsoft applications, such as Word, Excel, and PowerPoint. You have limited formatting capability with Pocket PC, but it's nice to be able to view and read documents without the need of your laptop or computer. Pocket PCs usually also have more multimedia applications available than do Palm OS models.

The popular BlackBerry models have their own operating system, the RIM OS. BlackBerry devices function similarly to the Palm OS systems. They have been the leader in providing units with email, Internet, and phone access. Large corporations and government agencies have been advocates of the BlackBerry system because the BlackBerry servers offer secure and private Internet and email access. These units can be more expensive than other handheld devices, though. If you think you will not use the BlackBerry for email, you might prefer a different and less-expensive model.

The following websites offer additional information about handhelds, including the latest reviews and newest models:

> **www.palminfocenter.com**—This site is an excellent source for current Palm industry news as well as software and hardware reviews.

> **www.pdabuyersguide.com**—This site is an independent site that offers advice on purchasing various handheld devices.

> **www.pdabuzz.com**—This site is an online publication that provides daily Palm and Pocket PC industry news as well as product reviews, editorials, and discussion boards.

> **www.pocketpcmag.com**—This site is an online publication that only discusses handheld issues. It offers a buyer's guide and a user's discussion forum.

> **www.pocketpcpassion.com**—This site is a resource page for Pocket PC's handheld devices.

Standard Handheld Features

The following are standard features and options you can choose from when purchasing most handhelds:

- **Memory**—If you are going to use your unit for the basic calendar, contact, and task features, you probably don't need much memory; 16MB–32MB of RAM will be fine. If you think you will want to save documents and download software or games, you probably should get at least 64MB of RAM or higher. If you are not sure, purchase a handheld that has the capability to upgrade memory in case you need it in the future.

- **Color versus green screen**—Color screens are nicer to view. They are also more expensive and sometimes harder to see in direct sunlight. Full-color screens also tend to use more battery power. Most green screens can run for more than a week without recharging.

- **Screen cover**—You should purchase a handheld that provides either a screen cover or a case. This protects the screen from scratches and helps prevent the unit from accidentally turning on and wasting battery power.

- **Keyboard versus handwriting recognition**—With handwriting recognition devices, you have to learn the graffiti style of writing with a pen-like stick called a *stylus*. This way of writing isn't difficult—it just requires some practice. If you feel learning the graffiti style is cumbersome, you might want to find a handheld with a small keyboard for typing characters, such as the Treo or BlackBerry. These keyboards can be difficult to use if you have large fingers, so you should test writing on both types of handheld devices before you purchase one.

  > **tip** Many people find that using a stylus or keyboard to enter data into handhelds can be awkward or seem intimidating. If this is the case for you, you can use your handheld as a reading tool to view your data that you have previously entered into your CM or PIM software. Carry a pad of paper and write down notes when you are away from your computer. Then, enter most of your data on your computer keyboard directly, if that seems easier than using the stylus or keyboard on the handheld.

- **Size**—Depending on where you are carrying your handheld, size and weight might make a difference. If you think you will want to carry it in your pocket, choose a lightweight device. If you are going to carry it in your day planner or a purse, take your day planner or purse with you when shopping to make sure the handheld fits well within it.

- **Battery life**—The newer models of handhelds all have a rechargeable battery system. Pocket PCs usually have a shorter battery life because of the operating system and color screen; these units typically run for a couple of days on a single charge. Most Palm OS units will last a few days, depending on how much you use them. If you use your handheld for more complex functions, such as Internet, phone, audio, games, or camera, you'll use up the battery charge faster. Buy a handheld that has a battery life long enough to manage the tasks you'll use it for most often.

- **Internet and email**—With most handhelds that connect to the Internet, you must subscribe to a separate ISP service to enable Internet access. Fees range from approximately $20 to $30 per month depending on the type of handheld and how frequently you use the Internet on your handheld. Most handhelds have the capability to save email on the server so you can download your email onto the handheld, read it, and delete it. Then when you get back to your office, you can download your email to your hard drive. This can be useful if you want to save your email in file folders on your hard drive. Some handhelds, such as the BlackBerry, have the capability to sync with your email manager and email file folders. You can file emails on your handheld in the appropriate file folder and the next time you sync, the handheld device automatically files the email in the file folder on your hard drive.

- **Document sync**—The Pocket PC systems have the capability to sync and view documents and attachments. This is useful if you have certain documents you want to access without the need of carrying your computer or paper copies. The system creates a separate file folder on your C drive for those documents you want to sync between your hard drive and handheld. You merely click and drag documents into this file folder and the next time you sync, they are accessible from your handheld.

> **note** I suggest creating copies of your documents, as opposed to moving them into the handheld file folder, so the original document stays in your primary file folder system on your hard drive. Also, be aware that the Palm OS platform does not automatically have the capability to view documents. However, if you download a third-party software called Documents To Go (www. wdocumentstogo.com), it will provide the capability to sync documents with your Palm OS handheld.

- **Cradle versus wireless sync**—Most handhelds sync using a standard USB cable that connects to your desktop or laptop computer. If you would rather not have a cable connection, consider purchasing a handheld with a wireless sync option.

- **Other features, such as camera, games, audio recording, and music**—All these other features take up considerable memory and battery power. I recommend purchasing a handheld with these features only if you really think you will use them. The camera can be useful if you need quick pictures, and the voice recording function can be useful if you like to tape meetings or capture thoughts vocally.

The following companies manufacture handheld devices:

- Palm (www.palmone.com)
- Handspring Visor (www.handspring.com)
- Sony (www.sony.com)
- Hewlett-Packard (www.hp.com)
- Dell (www.dell.com)
- Toshiba (www.toshiba.com)
- BlackBerry (www.blackberry.net)

Summary

In this chapter, you have learned how to use your contact manager or personal information management software to its full potential. Utilizing your CM and PIM can help you stay better organized and track your day-to-day information electronically. By tracking your calendar, contacts, and tasks electronically, I think you will find it easier to organize and plan your day more effectively. You've also learned how to create and use action lists and how to choose and use handheld devices to help keep your work day well-organized and functioning smoothly.

Following are some of the major action steps suggested in this chapter:

- Begin using your CM or PIM software system to its full potential by using the calendar, address book, and task functions.
- Enter all your business cards and contacts into your CM or PIM.
- Determine consistent tracking methods for your action items and consider tracking them in one location electronically.
- Purchase a handheld device so your CM and PIM data is always with you.

In the next chapter, "Hardcopy: Using a Paper Planner," we discuss how to purchase and use your paper planner effectively. We also discuss how you can coordinate your paper planner with your CM or PIM software tool.

Hardcopy: Using a Paper Planner

6

Electronic planning tools are not for everyone; if you like the look and feel of paper, then a paper planner/time management tool might be best for you. Some individuals like to use their trusty paper planners along with a handheld device. Thankfully, there are options for everyone.

The key to success with any time-management tool is consistency. If you determine to track your meetings and appointments in your paper planner and your contacts electronically, then remember to enter that information consistently in those locations. You'll run into problems if you record information about appointments, contacts, and action items in multiple places with no consistent plan for coordinating it. When this data becomes scattered and fragmented, tracking, organizing, and planning your day become difficult.

This chapter discusses how to use a paper planner effectively. To help you choose from among the many paper planner styles and designs, we discuss which format and size might be best for your needs. Because you can use your planner for much more than a calendar, we'll also look at all the other day-to-day information you can track in it. Many individuals cannot seem to function without their planners and would like to integrate

In this chapter:

* Learn how to choose a planner that is right for you

* Understand how to use your paper planner effectively

* Learn how to coordinate your handheld with your planner

them with a handheld or a contact management (CM) or personal information management (PIM) device. In this chapter, we discuss the best way to approach integrating electronic and paper planners.

To do list

- [ ] Determine the best size planner for you.
- [ ] Choose a calendar page format for your planner.
- [ ] Choose and set up note pages and sections in your planner.

Choosing a Planner

Paper planners are available both online and in office supply stores, and they come in a number of sizes, styles, and formats. Most planners are designed in a loose-leaf binder format, which makes customizing the planner to best suit your needs easy—an advantage not found in prebound planners. Paper planner pages are available in a wide variety of formats and layouts, so you can choose how you want to view your work week, daily appointments, contact information, and so on. The size of your planner also is important, and you can choose from among a large assortment here, as well. The size, color, materials, and page layout of your planner will determine how well it works for you and how likely you are to use it consistently. Before you purchase any planner, binder, or filler, ask yourself these questions:

- What kinds of information do I want to track in the planner, and is this format appropriate for that purpose?
- Does it have enough space and room to write the data I would like to capture?
- Will I use this kind of planner?
- Will I carry the planner with me?
- Is the planner's design appropriate to take to business meetings and appointments?

As I said, you have plenty of paper planners to choose from, so be sure you find one for which can answer "yes" to all these questions. The following sections talk about some of the variations you'll find in planner size and page layout to help you begin to narrow your choices.

Determining the Size

In choosing a planner, the first consideration is size. For time management tools to be effective, it is best if you carry your planner with you to meetings, to appointments, and out of the office. Therefore, it is important to have a size and weight that fits conveniently in your briefcase or bag. If your planner is too large, you might be reluctant to carry it with you, and therefore you won't use it effectively. If the planner is too small, you will find it hard to write—and read—the information you record in it. One of the main reasons individuals end up not using the paper planner they've purchased is because the planner wasn't the right size, so take care to choose a size that works best for you.

Although you can find planners in a variety of sizes, these three sizes are standard for paper planners:

- **Desktop**—The larger size, or *desktop*, paper planner is about 8" × 11", or the size of a standard piece of paper. This size is good for individuals who take a lot of daily notes and like to write on full sheets of paper. The larger size has enough space to write ample notes about calendar items, to-dos, and other events throughout the day. Because this is a standard paper size, you easily can add correspondence, memos, and other loose papers to your planner simply by using a three-hole punch on the documents. This is especially convenient for securing separate papers you need with you at meetings, at appointments, for projects, and so on. Because this size planner is larger and usually heavier to carry, I only recommend it for individuals who need to track a lot of information and are not in their offices or near a computer regularly. If you do purchase a desktop planner, you might consider getting a binder case that has a handle on it so you can carry it separately.

- **Classic**—The medium, or *classic*, size paper planner is usually about 5" × 7" and is similar to a small writing tablet. This size planner fits easily into a briefcase or bag, yet it's still large enough to give you room to write a good amount of daily notes. You can carry standard-sized paper in the planner by folding sheets in half and inserting them between regular planner pages. If you want to secure loose documents in the binder, you'll need to purchase a separate custom hole punch that matches the binder's size and ring configuration. This size planner is best for individuals who will be tracking all their day-to-day information in their planners and don't use an electronic CM or PIM software. It is also good for individuals who really want to track daily notes or phone calls on a calendar page.

- **Pocket**—The small, or *pocket*, size planner is about 3" × 5" and can fit into a small purse, bag, or suit pocket easily. This size is good if you want something light and easy to carry and don't need to record lots of appointment details or notes. This size isn't a good choice if your day is made up of a series of brief, back-to-back appointments; if you like to keep notes alongside your appointments; or if you want to carry a lot of loose papers and documents in your planner. This size is recommended only if you need a very basic calendar, task list, and address book.

Choosing the Page Type and Layout

With most paper planners, you can customize pages and inserts to fit your work needs. Most loose-leaf planners include inserts for calendar pages, address book and contact information pages, and notes pages. Most planner fillers also come bundled with other inserts, including reference information such as time zones, maps, dialing codes, and so on.

> **tip** Pocket-size planners are also good for individuals who have handhelds and want a basic calendar and note pages to carry with their handheld. It is much easier to view a monthly calendar in the pocket-size planner than on the handheld itself. It is also handy to track a few handwritten notes you might not want to enter into your handheld.

Many times, people buy planner inserts that they hope will be useful organizational tools, only to find that they just don't use them. Before you purchase additional pages and inserts, make sure you have a need for the types of space and information they offer. For example, if you track your contacts in a desktop flip-through card filer or handheld device, you might not need address book pages in your paper planner. If you determine that you would rather have your contacts in your planner, however, you might want to purchase address book pages and then transfer contact information into your paper planner.

How about your handwriting? If you write in large letters and like to have a lot of space to record information and notes, consider purchasing pages with ample blank space and note space. If you don't write many daily notes and have smaller handwriting, you will probably be fine with a limited notes area.

Calendar Pages

Most planners have either a one- or two-page format for daily, weekly, and monthly calendar pages. Individuals who have many daily appointments and like to write daily notes tend to purchase the daily page format. The daily two-page view is convenient for capturing all the information for that day in one place. You can use the right side page for appointments and action items; the left side page is usually blank so you can write phone messages, meeting notes, and all the other information received that day. The two-column page per day also provides a notes area, as shown in Figure 6.1. Having this page format can eliminate the need to track information in spiral tablets, note pads, sticky notes, or other small pieces of paper.

If you don't have a lot of weekly meetings and appointments (maybe only one or two per day) and like to view a week at a glance, you probably should get weekly view pages. I suggest purchasing the two-page format to give you enough room to write appointments and tasks without the pages looking too cluttered, as shown in Figure 6.2.

FIGURE 6.1

Shown here is a two-column, one-page daily format.

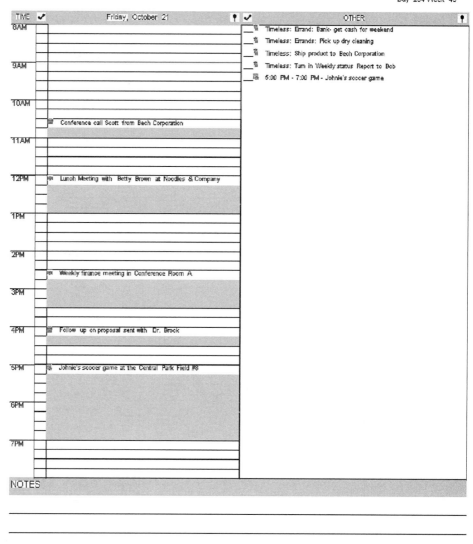

FIGURE 6.2

This calendar page shows an entire week on a single page.

17 October 20
Week 43

Monday 24
October 20

Monday, October 17	Thursday, October 20
	☎ 9:00 AM - 10:00 AM - Phone interview with prospective administrative
	⌨ 12:00 PM - 1:00 PM - Lunch meeting with Staff at Joe's Grill
	⌨ 1:00 PM - 2:00 PM - Weekly update - one on one
	⌨ 6:00 PM - 8:00 PM - Dinner meeting with George (discuss client proposal)

Tuesday, October 18	Friday, October 21
⌨ 11:00 AM - 12:00 PM - Monthly budget review meeting (Conference Room A)	☎ 10:00 AM - 11:00 AM - Conference call Scott Tom Tech Corporation
☎ 3:00 PM - 3:30 PM - Follow up with meeting with Elicia from last week	⌨ 12:00 PM - 1:00 PM - Lunch meeting with Betty Brown at Noodles & Company
	⌨ 2:00 PM - 3:00 PM - Weekly finance meeting in Conference Room A
	☎ 4:00 PM - 4:30 PM - Follow up on proposal sent with Dr. Brock

Wednesday, October 19	Saturday, October 22
	☎ Timeless: Follow-up with customer - product received
	Sunday, October 23
	⌨ 7:00 PM - 9:00 PM - Dinner Meeting

Monthly view pages, as shown in Figure 6.3, are nice to use in conjunction with daily or weekly pages. If you don't have many appointments, you might only need a monthly two-page view format. If you do choose to use the monthly format only, I suggest purchasing one that is at least 5" × 7" or bigger in size. This size gives you room to record appointments and take limited notes. If all you really need is a paper-based monthly calendar, then the smaller size will do fine.

September
S M T W T F S
1 2 3
4 5 6 7 8 9 10
11 12 13 14 15 16 17
18 19 20 21 22 23 24
25 26 27 28 29 30

October 2005

November
S M T W T F S
1 2 3 4 5
6 7 8 9 10 11 12
13 14 15 16 17 18 19
20 21 22 23 24 25 26
27 28 29 30

Sun	Mon	Tue	Wed	Thu	Fri	Sat
25	26	27	28	29	30	1
2	3	4	5	6	7	8
9	10	11	12	13	14	15
16	17	18	19	20	21	22
23	24	25	26	27	28	29
30	31	1	2	3	4	5

Address Book Pages

If you want your paper planner to be your primary address book, purchase address pages that allow 2" per contact to capture all the data for that person. I also suggest purchasing plastic business card holding pages and placing one plastic sheet between each alphabetical tab. That way, as you receive business cards, you can merely insert them into your address book. If you use a standard desktop business/address card filer as your primary system for your contacts and business cards, you might only need basic address pages in your planner to write down the frequent contacts you call.

Notes Pages

All sorts of note pages are available. Note pages can be plain or lined; other note pages are designed to track specific information such as meeting notes, projects, birthdays, task lists, phone calls/messages, and goals. You can use the preprinted pages to track this type of information or create your own lists using blank paper.

Most notes sections include tabbed dividers, which you can use to categorize and organize your notes. Creating notes sections helps you record and find information easily. Here are some of the sections you might use in your planner:

- **Projects**—Create a section for each major project that you have. You can keep important reference information, such as a project calendar or timeline, in this section. You can also track and store project meeting notes.

- **Meetings**—Create a section for each type of regular meeting you attend. Insert blank lined pages, and use them to track and keep meeting notes.

- **Clients**—Create a section for each of your clients. Then, all the phone communications, tasks, and meetings you have with each client are tracked and inserted into their designated sections. Creating client sections provides a notes and history section to track the status of each client's account and correspondence. If you have multiple clients, you can separate sections into broader categories such as by region or in an alphabetical range.

> **tip**   Be sure to date the top of each page of notes you keep in any of the notes sections of your planner. This way, when the next meeting or associated event occurs, you easily can find the notes from the previous meeting or event. Some individuals use their paper planners solely as a meeting notebook.

- **Departments and Colleagues**—If you participate in projects or other ongoing activities with a number of departments or colleagues, you can create sections for each of them and use those sections to track your progress and activities. Track the action items that each person or department has committed to, the meeting notes, and updates. When you need to follow up with that person or department, you have all the historical information in one section to review.

- **Reference**—Create sections for different types of reference that would be useful to have with you, such as schedules, phone lists, group calendars, maps, travel information, websites, and so on.

When you need to insert documents into this section, take the time to use your hole punch and insert them securely in your planner. This makes the information easily accessible and also ensures that the loose paper does not fall out of your planner. A little bit of time spent securing documents in the planner will save you a lot of time down the road when you don't have to search or backtrack for missing information.

PAPER PLANNER RECOMMENDATIONS

The following is a list of recommended paper planner manufacturers. You can order and learn more information about each product online:

- **AT-A-GLANCE (www.at-a-glance.com)**—The company began making desk calendars back in 1924. It has a broad range of calendars and day planners available at most office supply stores.

- **ClickBook (www.bluesquirrel.com/ clickbook)**—ClickBook is a software that allows you to design and customize your own paper planner using various layout designs.

- **Day Runner (www.dayrunner.com)**—You can order Day Runner products on its website or through your local office supply store. Its planner products are in a loose-leaf format and fit in ring binder notebooks.

- **Day-Timer (www.daytimer.com)**—One of the leading manufacturers of day planners, it offers a variety of pages, formats, and sizes. Day-Timer also has a nice online wizard that helps you create your own customized planner.

- **Digital Women (www.digital-women.com/daily planner)**—The Digital Women website provides free downloadable daily planner pages. These pages specifically track a wide range of information for the office and home.

- **FranklinCovey (www.franklincovey.com)**—FranklinCovey is one of the pioneers in time management systems and products. Its products are available online or through its retail stores.

- **Planner Pads Company (www.plannerpads.com)**—The Planner Pad is a prebound, one-page weekly view day planner. The planner has designated areas for a task list, projects, and daily appointments. This planner is standalone and cannot be customized with additional pages.

To do list

- ❏ Create a standard location for your paper planner on your desk.
- ❏ Carry your planner with you to meetings and appointments.
- ❏ Create and follow a consistent method for tracking information.
- ❏ Use codes and standard naming methods for appointments and tasks.
- ❏ Designate a specific location for loose paper in your planner.

Using Your Planner Effectively

Ideally, your day planner should always be located at your fingertips. If not, the information you need to track will be kept in your head or scribbled on pieces of paper; some of it will be unavailable when you need it, and some information will be lost entirely. You'll save time and effort by making a habit of always having your planner with you and avoiding the problems of finding and tracking information you gathered while away from your planner. Utilize your planner effectively by writing down information instantly when you receive it. After you write it down, you can forget it—no need to reenter it and no need to remember it. Your data is now safely in the appropriate area for you to retrieve and access it when you need it.

Like any organizing tool, a paper planner is only as good as the system for using it. If you determine that a paper planner is better for you than an electronic option, I recommend that you use it consistently.

Here are a few guidelines to help you get the most benefit from keeping and using your day planner:

- Create a standard place for your planner on your desk, such as beside your desk phone or computer, so you can quickly find and access that information.

- Make a rule that no paper or other articles get on top of your planner. That way, the planner is never out of sight or inaccessible when you need to record information. When your planner is conveniently located and visible, you're less likely to resort to writing appointments or phone numbers on sticky notes and floating pieces of paper.

- Take your planner with you to meetings and on business trips, but when you return to your office each day or after a meeting, be sure you always put your planner in the same location on your desk.

Not only can your planner save you time and effort, it can make you work *better*. In today's multitasking and information world, it is difficult to rely on memory. More than that, just like the computer, you are using up valuable short-term memory with your brain. The best time managers are those who don't rely on memory. They track information in a designated location to access when needed. Using your time management tool to track information gives you the power to forget. Then you have the full capacity of your thought and attention on the task, or conversation, at hand.

Things You'll Need

- ❑ Pen/pencil
- ❑ Your paper planner
- ❑ Color-coding markers or flags
- ❑ Clear vinyl sleeves for holding bills, directions, and other loose papers
- ❑ Group/shared calendar

Keeping Personal, Business, and Group Calendars

You'll enter all scheduled appointments and meetings on your planner's calendar pages. Ideally it is best to have one calendar on which you track both personal and business-related appointments and meetings. Keeping one calendar is simpler than using multiple calendars, and it leaves less room for errors and oversights. When you have more than one personal calendar, you have to be careful of recording the same information in multiple places. And, inevitably, you forget to track the data in both locations and then scheduling conflicts can occur. Rectifying scheduling conflicts takes time and can be difficult. If you feel you must keep separate business and personal calendars, make sure both are located in your paper planner and easily accessible.

> **tip** Add in cushions of time in your day. If you regularly schedule back-to-back appointments, consider planning in 10–15 minute increments so you have time to check voice mail, return phone calls, and track information in your hand-held or planner. This helps you stay organized and current with routine tasks. Leaving time between appointments also can help prevent one late-running meeting from bumping your schedule out for the rest of the day.

If you have electronic group or shared calendars, you can print them and put them in your planner. You might want to create a separate section for each type of calendar. Or you can merely insert the calendars under the appropriate month or week tab.

Entering Appointments and Events

Create a standard naming format for calendar entries in your planner for easy viewing. Determine which types of meetings and appointments you want to be most immediately visible on your calendar; then determine a code, symbol, color, or standard subject name that will make those entries stand out. You can use colored pens or highlighters to color-code appointments. You also can use any of a number of coding options to identify specific types of appointments. If you have a busy schedule and record all business and personal appointments and events on a single calendar, coding is a fast and simple method for noting (and recalling) important information about each of those items. Here are a few examples of appointment/event codes, some of which are shown in Figure 6.4:

- **Personal versus business**—To quickly view personal versus business appointments, you can use a code or color to distinguish between them. For example, put the letters *PSL* before the appointment entry to signify a personal appointment, and possibly the letters *BIZ* for business appointments.

- **Tentative meetings**—If you have a tentative meeting, use the letters *TNT* behind the entry to signify that it is not confirmed and tentative. After it's confirmed, you could cross out the *TNT* and write *CFD* to symbolize it has been confirmed.

- **Reoccurring appointments**—I suggest that you take the time to write these in your calendar a few months (or weeks) in advance so you don't forget them. By marking them with a code, such as with the letter *R*, you give yourself a visual reminder to reschedule that appointment for the next occurrence.

- **Annual events**—For annual holidays, events, and birthdays, it is best to track these appointments in a monthly view as well as in your daily or weekly view. Consider highlighting these events to distinguish them from regular meetings. With birthdays, you could use the code *BD* and write the person's name behind it—for example, *BD-Linda*.

> **tip** If you created a separate birthday list, write in your planner on the first day of the month to check the birthday list for that month. Do the same for holidays and events. This way you can preplan gifts, cards, arrangements, or phone calls that you need to take action on.

- **Family members**—If you need to track appointments for other members of your family, you can place that family member's name within the recorded item. For example, *Sally-Piano Lesson* reminds you of both the event and the family member who'll participate in it.

Managing Loose Paper

There will always be separate or loose paper that you will want to carry with you in your planner. Here are some suggestions of possible locations for common paper items:

FIGURE 6.4

You can use standard naming conventions to code various types of meetings and appointments in your paper planner, so you'll recognize the nature of the appointment at a glance.

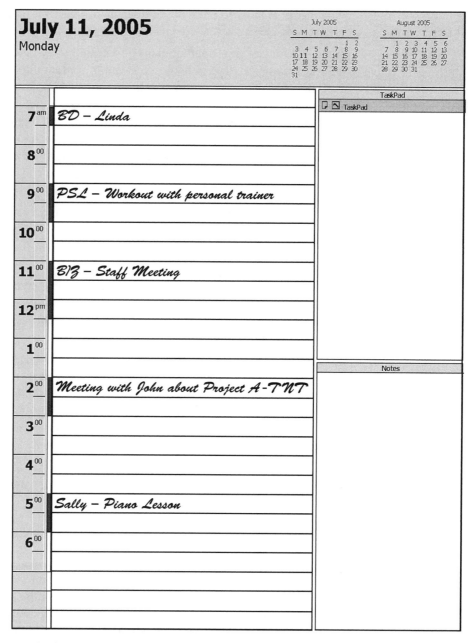

- **Action items**—Insert paper action items inside your planner next to the day, week, or month you intend to take the action. If you would rather not carry the additional paper, write down that action item on the day or week you want to accomplish the task; also mark where you have stored the corresponding paper. You can also designate a section in your planner solely for paper action items. (You learn more about tracking action items in the next sections of this chapter.)

- **Email**—If many of your appointments and meetings are determined and confirmed via email, the email messages might contain important details about those events. You can copy the information from the email into your paper planner, or you can print the email and insert it in your paper planner. If the latter option results in printing, carrying, and organizing too much paper, keep the email messages in your electronic inbox and mark the date of the message and the sender's name or initials next to the appropriate calendar items. That way, on that day of the meeting, you can quickly locate the email and review the details or print it for that day's meeting.

- **Bills**—If you want to keep bills in your planner to remind you to pay them, create a specific area to keep them, such as in the front or back pocket of the planner. Or purchase a separate plastic sleeve, insert it in the appropriate section of your planner, and keep pending bills within it.

- **Coupons**—Create one designated area to keep coupons in your planner. Usually a separate plastic sleeve that opens from the top or side is best. If you have a tendency to forget that you have coupons in your planner, carry coupons in your wallet instead.

- **Directions**—If you have an area to track notes on your calendar page, write the directions directly on the notes page. If not, use a sticky note to write down the directions and then place the sticky note on that day or week page. If you have the directions in an email, print the email and insert it in your planner. Or, write the date of the email and the sender's name next to the appointment and print the email directions when that day arrives.

- **Invitations**—It is best to insert the invitation in the day or week that the event is scheduled. Either paper clip the invitation to the page or hole punch and insert it directly into the planner.

Tracking Action Items

Action items are tasks or to-do's that you must accomplish. With most calendar pages, there is a sidebar or area to track action items. You can also track tasks on separate note pages located within your planner. Remember to assign due dates to all tasks. Write tasks on the calendar page of the date you want to take action. If you track your action items separately on note pages, be sure to write a due date next to the task.

You can use your planner's calendar to track action items in a number of ways, depending on your preferences and your calendar's page layout.

Most daily page view calendars have a designated to do column for tracking action items. Enter your action items on the day you want to take action and then check off the items after you complete them. The action items you do not complete need to be moved forward to the day of your choosing; code these listings (refer to "Entering Appointments and Events," earlier in this chapter), so you know they have been moved forward, rather than completed or overlooked. Use a capital *M* to signify moved, or use another code or symbol of your choosing. Instead of moving tasks forward daily, you can wait and move them forward weekly, if you prefer.

On most weekly view pages, there is a to do column or area located on the left side or at the bottom of the page. When you track action items in a weekly view, you typically don't assign a specific due date but are simply listing the tasks you must complete within that week. For some, a weekly action list is ample and daily due dates simply aren't necessary. If you would like to distinguish dates for each task, write the date or day abbreviation next to the action item. In any case, listing tasks in order of their priority can help you determine which tasks to tackle first.

If you do not have a designated to-do area in your week view planner, you can create one. One option is to track all weekly action items on a large sticky note and place it on the side of the page. Another option is to track action items in an unused time interval of each day's listing in your weekly view. You might want to use the 6:00 a.m. to 8:00 a.m. slot, for example, or 8:00 p.m. to 10:00 p.m. area to track your action items. Creating and using a daily action list in your weekly view can be useful.

Most monthly view pages don't have a designated to-do column or area. It is best to have a separate page as your action list if you have a monthly view planner. When creating action lists on separate paper from your calendar, remember to track deadline dates and priorities with each task. This helps determine which task items to perform first. Keep your action list in front of your monthly calendar so you can see it easily.

caution Avoid tracking tasks on sticky notes. Sticky notes lose their stickiness and become lost, or they get piled on top of one another or stuck between other papers, where they become useless as visible reminders. If you can't break the habit of using sticky notes to record task reminders, insert the sticky note in your planner on the day or week you intend to do the task. Then, the tasks will be consolidated in your planner and also be assigned a due date. If you track only immediate doable tasks on sticky notes, be sure to recycle the sticky note directly after completing the task.

THE $3 PLANNER

If you find paper planners and electronic software are too complicated for your needs, consider keeping your schedule in a plain, empty spiral notebook. For a few dollars, you can have a simple paper planner to track your day-to-day information. The empty notebook can become your daily log of notes, including action items, meeting notes, phone log, and reference. Any information you write down will be tracked chronologically in this notebook. I suggest dating the top of each page so you have a way to easily refer to items. I also suggest coding or highlighting action items, so you can spot them easily on the page. For some, this method is easier than having different views, pages, and locations for day-to-day information. If you find that you like this method, consider upgrading to a hardback empty notebook. If you use this method to track your schedule, you might want to keep your calendar electronically and print it as needed or have a separate monthly calendar that fits inside the notebook.

To do list

☐ Create a clear distinction of which types of information you will track in your planner and electronic tool.

☐ Print information from your CM or PIM and insert into your planner.

Coordinating Your Planner with Your Handheld

Today most individuals prefer to use some combination of electronic and paper-based time management tools. The benefit of using an integrated electronic and paper planning system is that it enables you to track data in the format that is most useful and comfortable for you. Some individuals prefer to record certain kinds of information by hand but like having other data in electronic form. You might, for example, decide to maintain your calendar and daily notes in a paper planner while using a PDA to handle tasks and contact/address information. If you have considered moving to an electronic time management tool but don't feel quite ready to toss your paper planner completely, you might want to use a combination system while you're transitioning to the new planner style.

The keys to using both systems are to clearly delineate which kind of information is tracked in which tool and to have and consistently use a plan for coordinating the two parts of the system. This approach becomes complicated when you fall into the habit of tracking the same information in both locations. For example, one day you write an appointment in your planner, but the next day you write appointments in your handheld. Inconsistency creates confusion and makes it difficult to plan and organize your day. Keep in mind, too, that you'll need to maintain two systems— electronic and paper—which can take more energy and effort than what's required to maintain a single system.

Here are some common handheld and paper planner combinations that might work for you:

- Handheld: Address book

  Paper planner: Calendar, meeting and daily notes, action list

  Good for: Individuals who are just beginning to use a handheld. Start with tracking your address book first and use your paper planner for everything else. Then, slowly you can add more functions electronically as you feel more comfortable using your handheld.

- Handheld: Calendar and address book

  Paper planner: Action list, meeting and daily notes

  Good for: Individuals who have a handheld and need to track their calendars electronically for other colleagues to see, but still like to handwrite information and aren't completely comfortable writing a lot of notes into a handheld.

- Handheld: Calendar, address book, and task list

  Paper planner: Meeting and daily notes

  Good for: Individuals who are using their CM and PIM software tool completely and would like to have that information available to them when they're away from their desks or offices; many people prefer to handwrite meeting and daily notes.

- Handheld: Business calendar, address book, task list

  Paper planner: Personal calendar, address book, task list

  Good for: Individuals who have a lot of information to track on a personal/family and business level and would like to track the data on separate time management systems. Tracking personal information in a paper-based format can be more convenient for those individuals with families and children on the go.

Things You'll Need

- ☐ Printer
- ☐ Paper-based planner
- ☐ PDA or other electronic time-management tool
- ☐ CM or PIM software, such as Outlook, ACT!, GroupWise, Palm, or Lotus Notes

Setting Up a System

Determine which location (electronic or planner) will be the primary tracking location for your appointments, contact information, tasks, and daily notes. For instance, if you determine that you'll track calendar items electronically, be sure to enter all calendar items into your electronic time-management tool. If you handwrite additional appointments on the calendar pages of your paper-based planner, always make sure that by the end of each day you have entered all such appointments electronically. The same rule applies to all items and information you keep in your time-management tools. Designate which information belongs in which tool, and follow that designation consistently. Consider checking both tools weekly to make sure you have transferred and entered data correctly.

> **tip** Some planner cases have specific areas to hold your handheld. Test your handheld in that designated area, to make sure you can access the buttons, keys, and stylus easily. Because you will need to sync your handheld regularly, be sure to check that your handheld slides easily in and out of the designated slot.

Printing Electronic Elements in Paper Planner Formats

Most CMs and PIMs allow you to print your calendar, address book, and task list in standard paper planner formats with multiple print options. This approach lets you view your information electronically and on paper; it also enables you to quickly and easily transfer large amounts of information from your electronic planner to your paper-based planner. You can simply print the elements, prepare them with your hole punch, and then clip them in your planner binder.

Print options are usually found under the Print menu of your CM or PIM software. In Microsoft Outlook, under the Print menu, you can print your calendar in daily, weekly, or monthly views. Click in the Calendar folder and select File, Print. Once in the Print window, select your preferred calendar format under the Print Style options, as shown in Figure 6.5. In the Start and End text boxes of the Print Range area, choose the date range you want to print. Click Page Setup to open a separate window with further print options.

FIGURE 6.5

When printing cal-
endar pages in
Microsoft Outlook,
click the Preview
button before you
print; that way you
can make sure
you've chosen the
format and date
range you want to
print.

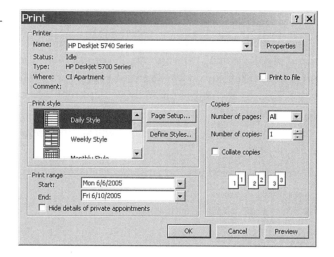

FIGURE 6.5

When printing cal-
endar pages in
Microsoft Outlook,
click the Preview
button before you
print; that way you
can make sure
you've chosen the
format and date
range you want to
print.

You also can print calendar pages in ACT!, as
shown in Figure 6.6. In the Print menu, select
File, Print. Once in the Print window, select what
you want to print from the Printout Type option
drop-down list. Then, highlight the type of day
planner and view style you prefer. If you click
Options, a separate window opens with further
print options, including date range. Click OK to
finish.

Again, if you handwrite additional information
on the printed calendar, address book, or task
lists, be diligent about updating your CM and
PIM with that information. Using this combination tracking system is helpful only if you remember to update both parts of the system regularly.

tip

Display your name and contact
information clearly in the front
of the planner, in case it's lost or stolen and
later recovered. And don't let any portable
device—paper or electronic—be the sole
keeper of important and irreplaceable data.
Periodically photocopy important information, such as your address book, and store it
in a safe location. Syncing your handheld
device with a desktop computer is a good
way to maintain an ongoing backup of your
electronic data.

FIGURE 6.6

In ACT!, you can
choose to print your
calendar using a
number of paper
planner formats.

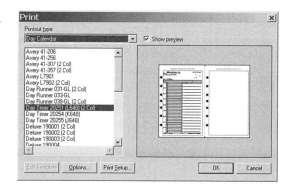

Summary

In this chapter, you have learned how to choose and use your paper planner more effectively to track your day-to-day information. Paper planners are useful tools to track daily information, either in conjunction with your CM or PIM software or as standalone devices. The key with any time-management tool is to maintain consistency in tracking and using it.

Here are some of the important recommendations you should remember from this chapter:

- Determine which size planner and pages you need based on the daily information you track.
- Regularly carry your planner with you.
- Begin to code your appointments and action items, as needed.
- Consider using a handheld in conjunction with your paper planner.
- Be consistent with tracking information in the designated area in your planner.

In the next chapter, "Improving Your Relationship with Email," you learn how and why to back up your key electronic data, and how doing so can help you get the most from your work day. We also discuss which backup options are available and which options will work best for you.

Part III

Managing Daily Tasks

Improving Your Relationship with Email

The number of emails sent on an average day is expected to exceed 36 billion worldwide in 2005. It is also estimated that more than 60% of business-critical information resides on email systems. Email is now the primary source of communications and information sharing in the workplace, so it's vital to be efficient and organized with all email correspondence if you want to have a well-organized work day.

No matter how important it is, you can't afford to let email consume your work day. The compelling feeling that you have to stop your current action and read the incoming email at the very moment it is

note Many types of email software programs are available. The most commonly used email programs are personal information managers (such as Outlook, Entourage, Lotus Notes, or GroupWise) discussed in Chapter 5, "Using Your Contact Software to Its Full Potential." Most email programs have the basic functions we discuss in this chapter. If you are unsure how to access those functions, consult your computer consultant or the Help tool in your program. The examples shown in this chapter were done in Outlook 2003 using the Windows XP operating system. Some of the directions and instructions might vary slightly if you have earlier versions of the software or PC operating system.

In this chapter:

* Learn ways to reduce the time you spend managing email
* Create a three-part email management plan
* Discover how to use filters, rules, and multiple accounts to help keep your inbox clean
* Understand the benefits of not printing email
* Create an email file system

received can translate into a huge time-waster. Email needs to be *one* of your priorities, with its management scheduled along with other tasks you need to complete each day.

In this chapter, you learn how to develop an email management system that helps you keep on top of email without neglecting other important tasks. We are going to discuss how to develop and manage email communications effectively. You learn how to efficiently compose email, set and manage an effective response schedule, keep your inbox clean, and organize an archive and filing system for messages.

To do list

- ❑ Set time limits for responding to email.
- ❑ Compose emails that encourage the recipient to read and respond.

Spending Your Whole Day Doing Email?

Eight o'clock, Monday morning—you turn on your computer, open your email software, move the mouse, and click the Send/Receive button. The download of new messages starts slowly and then becomes a flood. When it stops, your inbox is full of new messages and there you are—another day, drowning in email.

Employees at most businesses receive an average of 50 email messages daily and usually need a minimum of 2 hours to manage them. However, the famous Parkinson's law states that work will expand to fill the time available for completion. So, if you let email take your whole day, it will. To maximize your day, it is important to determine a plan for when and how often you'll deal with email each day, and how much time you need daily to manage email effectively.

Things You'll Need

- ❑ Primary email software
- ❑ Master outline, created in Chapter 3

Setting Email Time Limits

Why do we feel the need to look at email constantly? That is the question each person needs to address to become more efficient at email. After you recognize your email habits, you can make a conscious choice of how best to address and alter them to maximize your day. You might have one or more of these reasons for constantly checking your email:

- You have reason to expect to receive urgent or important email.
- The corporate culture in which you work encourages immediate viewing of all email information.
- Email is central to your job.
- You don't want to miss anything.
- Email is easy to view and respond to, and therefore is a good way to avoid other priorities that might require more concentration or time.

If you allowed yourself to do so, you could spend the entire day reading and responding to email. But if you don't want email to serve as a major interruption within your work day, you can designate a schedule for checking and responding to email messages. That way, you can spend more time concentrating on other important action items.

Your job will have its own unique requirements for how frequently you need to view and respond to email. As a general rule, you might be able to check email as few as two or three times a day—in the morning, after lunch, and before leaving at the end of the day. You might need to schedule more or fewer times for managing email, but the important thing is to determine how frequently you need to view email and then to set up and follow a regular and consistent schedule. Your goal is to avoid spending your entire day reading and responding to emails; developing an email schedule can be one way to guard against that habit.

As discussed in Chapter 1, "Knowing What You Want from Your Work Day," it is important to determine your best times of day for managing this kind of task. When making this decision, consider when email management fits best within your job activities and daily schedule. It has become accepted corporate culture to check email first thing in the morning, and this might be your habit. If that truly is the best time for you to check email, continue with that habit. You might find, however, that responding to phone calls or other top priorities might be more appropriate items to handle first thing in the

> **tip**
>
> During the time of day that you are not managing email, consider turning off your new email alert function when you receive an email. This prevents your attention from being taken away from current tasks-at-hand to read that new email. Or consider closing the email program entirely to focus your attention on other priorities. This way, you won't be tempted to get caught up in email when you are working on other action items.

morning. If that's the case, you might want to schedule your first email check at mid-morning. By setting an email schedule that fits your preferences, you are taking control of your workday, rather than letting it be controlled by email.

Of course, your schedule might vary occasionally to accomodate meetings, appointments, and other issues that arise during your day. And, if your email correspondents are accustomed to getting immediate responses from you, you should let everyone know that you've adopted a new email schedule. You might, for example, send out a message explaining your schedule and letting correspondents know that they can expect a response from you within 24 hours (unless you are out of the office). Also, let colleagues and clients know how to best reach you with urgent matters or emergencies—for example, by telephone rather than email.

Composing Email Effectively

Unfortunately, time is wasted reading and responding to poorly written or ambiguous emails. It is important when composing emails to be clear and concise and to write your messages in a manner that encourages the recipient to read and respond to them quickly. The art of effective composition of emails is key to maximizing your time as well as your recipients'. Describing the key content in an email subject line, writing a concise and easy-to-read message, and clearly outlining the response you need from your recipients increase your chances of a quick response.

Creating Clear Subject Lines

Write a subject line that completely describes the content of your message. Describe key information in the subject line so that the recipient can determine what the subject matter is at the first glance. For instance, if you are planning a meeting and notifying others via email, instead of using a one-word subject line such as "meeting," consider adding the date, time, and type of meeting—for example, "Staff Meeting - Monday, November 14th at 9:00 a.m." Having an appropriate subject line is also important for future retrieval to remember the content of the email.

If the email content and subject matter change after a few exchanges, be sure to change the subject line too. This alleviates opening multiple emails with the same subject heading with different topics discussed. The more clear, detailed, and accurate you make your subject lines, the easier it will be to sort, file, and retrieve those messages later—and the more likely your recipients are to read and respond to your messages accurately and quickly.

Composing Standard Signatures

Create an automatic email signature with your name and contact information, and use it every time you write an email. This saves you time and eliminates the need to check the spelling or accuracy of this information. Standard signatures also signify professionalism with business email. A standard signature should include the following information: full name, title, company name, phone, fax, mailing address, email address, and website address. Most email programs have an automatic signature feature located under the email options or preference functions (see Figure 7.1). When you've created a standard signature in Outlook, it appears automatically in all new message windows.

FIGURE 7.1

A sample signature developed in the Create Signature window in Microsoft Outlook. To create a standard signature for all outgoing email in Outlook, select Tools, Options and click the Mail Format tab. Then click the Signatures button and click the New button to open the Create New Signature dialog box. Follow the instructions in that dialog box to finish your signature.

Composing Brief and Concise Emails

Try to keep all email messages short and concise; one page or less is best. If it takes longer than 2–3 minutes to read your email, consider deleting some content. Keeping your email brief encourages the recipient to read it immediately. When emails become too long, individuals might skip over your email to another email that is shorter. After an email is skipped, it becomes less likely a reader will return to your email because of the daily flood of email in everyone's inbox.

Keep the email concise and tell the reader what you need; clearly state what action or decision is required of the recipient(s) and give a recommended deadline to respond. This information should be located in the first few sentences or paragraph of the email. Use formatting to make the email easier to read. Use bold, underline, bullets, and numbering as appropriate to highlight separate issues. Most email programs have a formatting toolbar located in a new message window. In Outlook, if you do not see the formatting toolbar, choose View, Toolbars, Formatting to display the Formatting

tip

When possible, limit email messages to a single subject. This helps you and your recipients focus on the essential topic, keeps messages short, and aids in finding and referencing specific email messages.

toolbar. You do not have to repeat this step again; the formatting toolbar will automatically be inserted when you open a new email message again.

Consider reusing email messages as templates for frequently sent messages to avoid retyping similar content each time. Most email software has the capability to save an email and then retrieve it later for reuse. In Microsoft Outlook, you can actually create email templates; follow these steps:

1. Open a new email message window and type the subject line and body text of the template email message.

2. Select File, Save As to open the Save As window.

3. In the Save As File Type drop-down box, select Outlook Template.

4. Type in a filename for the email message template. Click Save.

5. In Outlook, select File, New, Choose Form to open the Choose Form window, as shown in Figure 7.2.

6. Open the Look in drop-down list, and select User Templates in File System. Then, highlight your email message template file from the listing shown in the box below and click Open.

7. A new email message appears with the template email text shown. Enter the recipient's email address and add text to change the template as needed; then send the email when finished.

note Check to make sure you are not using Word to edit your email messages; otherwise, you will not be able to perform the stepped instructions for saving an email as a template. In Outlook, select Tools, Options. Then, in the Mail Format tab, be sure to deselect the Use Microsoft Word to Edit Email Messages and Use Microsoft Word to Read Rich Text Email Messages check boxes. Click OK to close the Options dialog box, and you are then ready to follow the steps for creating an email template. The Microsoft Word Mail Format options also must be deselected for you to access the email template.

tip If the sender asked a series of questions in the body of the email, respond to those questions in bold or colored text just after the question. This technique is faster, easier, and more efficient than rewriting the questions in a separate response. Be sure you reply to the email with the *history*, or the text of the email, included in the response. Type a quick "See responses with your individual questions below." Then, write your responses just after the sender's questions in bold or color text.

FIGURE 7.2
In Microsoft Outlook you use the Choose Form dialog box to select your email template. Highlight the email template and then click Open.

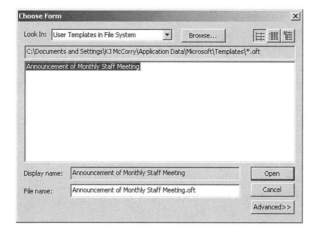

DEVELOPING EMAIL POLICIES

If your company does not have an email policy, you might want to develop one for your organization or division. An email policy can help everyone in the department manage email more efficiently, and it helps to ensure consistent and professional email communications. The following websites can provide more information about how to create an effective set of email policies:

- **The ePolicy Institute (www.epolicyinstitute.com/ index.shtml)**—This site offers books on how to develop email policies. They also have a good do's and don'ts list of implementing email policies.

- **Computer Professionals for Social Responsibility (www.cpsr. org/program/emailpolicy.html)**—This site provides a sample email policy for companies.

- **Email Policy (www.email-policy.com)**—This site provides sample email policies. It also recommends books and software that provide information on email policy development.

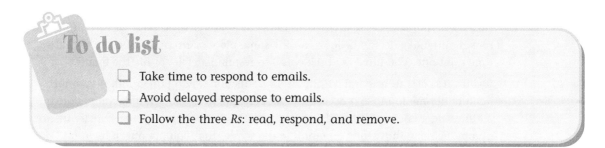

To do list

- ☐ Take time to respond to emails.
- ☐ Avoid delayed response to emails.
- ☐ Follow the three *Rs*: read, respond, and remove.

Following the Three *R*s of Efficient Email: Read, Respond, and Remove

To manage email effectively apply the three *R* rule—read, respond, and remove. After you open an email, do the following:

1. Read it entirely.

2. Respond to the email.

3. Remove the message from your inbox by deleting or filing it.

When you manage email in this fashion, you have to deal with that email only once and can move on to the next email. This approach reduces inbox clutter, encourages immediate response and action, and eliminates the need to reread emails (either for response or filing). Just as no one wants to file a huge stack of papers, no one wants to reread and file a long list of email messages. Don't put yourself in that position; begin to use the three *R*s rule of email management.

> **tip** If a series of emails has been written and the issue or problem has not been resolved in three or four emails, consider talking with the person directly, by phone, or in a meeting to resolve the issue. Remember that email is a communications tool, but not a replacement for direct verbal communication in all situations.

Avoiding the Traps of Delayed Response

Many of the problems in managing email result from delayed response and action. These problems result when recipients open and read (or skim through) an email message, click and skim the next message, and so on, failing to act on or respond to any message before moving on to the next. By quickly scanning email and not dealing with it immediately, you're ensuring that you'll have to open and read the message at least once more, thereby doubling the amount of time required for the first step in handling the message. And frequently, you fail to remember or return to the message at all. Email keeps coming every minute of every day, and rarely do most individuals have time to go back and reread past messages. This skim-and-delay technique is an inefficient and ineffective way to manage email communications.

Like other important communication tasks, respond to email immediately when possible. Delaying your reply after scanning your email is lost time because you have to reread and make decisions again on the same piece of email. It is best to take the time right after you have read the email to respond, delete, or file the email.

Ideally, it is best to respond within 24–48 hours of receiving an email. If you need additional time to make a decision or take action, give yourself a deadline date and let the sender know about it. If you are out of town, it is appropriate to activate an automatic reply that sends an email to the sender that you are out of town and when you expect to respond to emails.

To set up an automatic reply for personal email accounts, you usually need to go through your Internet service provider account options or preferences. If you are on a networked server system and use a company-wide email program, you can usually set up an automatic reply through the user options and preference tools within the software. For Outlook users who are on a Microsoft Exchange Server network, follow these directions:

1. In the Tools menu, select Out of Office Assistant. (Note: This option is not present unless you are on a Microsoft Exchange Server network.)

2. Click in the I Am Currently Out of the Office text box, and type the message you want senders to automatically receive. I suggest letting senders know you are out of the office and when you expect to return, along with another contact name, email, or phone number to contact with urgent business.

3. Click OK to close the Out of Office Assistant window.

Set aside an appropriate amount of time to read, respond, and manage your email. If you find that you frequently don't have enough time to deal with email as you open it, consider changing your email schedule to a time that permits you to manage your messages.

Flagging Email for Follow-up

Regardless of how carefully you schedule your times, occasionally you won't be able to respond immediately to an email message. In such cases, or when you need to take a later follow-up action, use these techniques for keeping that follow-up on your to-do list:

- **Move the email to your electronic (or paper) task list**—With most CMs and PIMs, you can copy an email into an

caution In some circumstances, it is best to not respond to email right away. Some emails you receive can cause you to feel angry or upset; others might require some fact-checking before you can respond accurately. In those situations, you might want to delay your response to ensure that it really communicates the message you need to send. Even if you type a response immediately, if you're feeling at all angry or uncertain about the message, save your email as a draft and make a note to yourself to return to it later. After you've had sufficient time to consider your response, reread the email and make any necessary changes before sending it. More often than not, the revised email version will be less emotional, more professional, and a better version of the information you want and need to convey. Don't let email's ease and speed seduce you into writing something you regret. Take time to respond to delicate situations thoughtfully to save embarrassment, frustration, or further confusion and hard feelings.

caution If you choose to use an Action folder to house action-related email, you have to be extremely diligent to review this folder daily. Otherwise, the action items will be forgotten. This is recommended only if you find it easier to manage action items in a separate file folder. Most individuals are more likely to take action if the email stays in their inbox.

electronic task within the software. This does not remove the email from your inbox; it merely copies the email into the task list. Then, you can schedule the task/email follow-up for a future date. The email itself then can be deleted or moved to the appropriate file folder.

- **Flag or keep email as unread—** Inserting the flag icon or keeping email as unread signifies that email still needs action taken. Most email software programs have various options to flag email that you can use to clearly identify priority email messages.

- **Keep the email in your inbox—**Refrain from moving emails from your inbox until action has been taken. If an email is still located in your inbox, you know some sort of action must be taken.

- **Create a file folder called Action—**You can move all action-related emails into this folder.

caution When you don't respond to an email or task request you have agreed to do, you have tacitly made a decision of no response. By avoiding the decision of an action, you are in fact forcing others to make decisions on your behalf. This also affects your colleagues who will assume decisions that you might not want them to assume. For instance, if you don't respond to a meeting invitation, the sender can assume a multitude of reasons such as you aren't available, you are upset, you don't care, or you don't consider it a priority. Maybe one of the assumptions is true and maybe none of them are. By lack of response, the sender is left to determine the reason for himself.
These assumptions usually cause friction and communication issues within the workplace.

EMAIL PROTOCOL

With email replacing phone and face-to-face conversations, it is crucial to write clear and legible emails. It is also important to consider which types of issues you should send via email and which issues you should communicate verbally. Remember these standard email protocol guidelines:

- **Check spelling and grammar**—Be sure to check spelling, grammar, and punctuation before you send business email. Consider activating your automatic spell checker, which is usually located under the Preferences or Options section of your email program. You would not send a cover letter on company letterhead with incorrect grammar or spelling, so don't do it with email communications either.

- **Refrain from forwarding nonessential email**—Don't waste your time (or the company's resources) forwarding jokes, inspiration, chain letters, or virus warnings on to business colleagues. Because of the mass amount of these types of email, and the uncertainty of their origins, it is considered inappropriate email etiquette to forward these types of emails.

- **CC and BCC appropriately**—Only send an email by CC or BCC to those individuals who really need to see the email. If you are CC'd or BCC'd on an email, you are not expected to respond.

If you are sending information to more than 15 individuals, you should BCC all members so the recipients can view the message easily without scrolling through a list of CC email names.

- **Refrain from using emoticon characters**—Emoticons are smiley faces and other keyboard characters used to convey anger, laughter, and other emotions. There are hundreds of such characters, and their translations are not universal in meaning. Instead of using emoticons in business email, write directly what you would like to express.

- **Be mindful of what you write**—Many individuals mistake email for being a private communication tool. The challenge with email is that you never know after you send it to someone who that person will then send it on to. So, be careful what you write in any email message, and be sure you don't write anything that might come back to haunt you either personally, professionally, or legally.

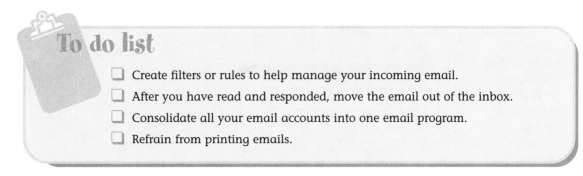

To do list

- ❏ Create filters or rules to help manage your incoming email.
- ❏ After you have read and responded, move the email out of the inbox.
- ❏ Consolidate all your email accounts into one email program.
- ❏ Refrain from printing emails.

Managing the Inbox

If you can manage your inbox effectively, you will be a successful email and time manager. The key is to keep your inbox free of messages other than those you need to take action on or have not opened. This arrangement requires that you create a home for all other emails.

Using the filter or rule function in your email software helps you manage your inbox. You can assign certain reoccurring emails to go to a designated location automatically. This can be useful for email such as spam, newsletters, updates, and so on.

The key to setting up an email filing and archiving system is to have clear designations for all types of emails you receive. All emails are types of actions, as discussed in depth in Chapter 5. With each email action, you should develop a plan of management.

Creating Filters and Rules

Filters or *rules* examine incoming messages for user-specified conditions and respond with specified actions. Use filters or rules functions (the term varies from software to software, but both describe the same thing) to help with the initial sort of incoming email.

The Microsoft Outlook Rules Wizard dialog box is shown in Figure 7.3. Filter and rule functions automatically move or delete unwanted mail before it reaches your inbox. For example, you can determine that all email messages containing a certain subject heading should be deleted before entering your inbox or that email from a particular sender be automatically moved into a specified folder. When you set up a rule or filter, the incoming email is redirected to a different file folder and is diverted from your inbox entirely.

FIGURE 7.3

The Rules Wizard in Microsoft Outlook. To open the Rules Wizard, select Tools, Rules and Alerts; then click the New Rule icon to open the Rules Wizard window. Select one of the options listed in step 1 and click Next. When you're finished creating the rule, be sure you have marked the rule as activated by clicking in the box next to the rule.

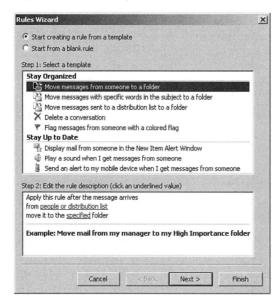

Setting up rules and filters can be useful in the following situations:

- **Reducing spam or unsolicited email**—If you receive unsolicited email, you can create a rule or filter to delete emails from certain addresses or containing certain subject headings.

- **Sorting mail sent through distribution lists**—If you receive certain emails that are company updates and newsletters, you could move them to an email file folder called Newsletters or To Read and then review them during a designated time during the week.

- **Projects**—If you have certain project communications and updates that don't require any action on your part, you can move them directly to a project file folder.

GETTING RID OF SPAM EMAIL

By 2006, consumers are expected to receive an average of 1,400 pieces of junk mail in their email inboxes each year. The U.S. Senate Committee on Commerce, Science and Transportation has approved S.877 Controlling the Assault of Non Solicited Pornography and Marketing Act of 2003 (CAN-SPAM Act). The act allows consumers to opt out of unwanted commercial email messages, commonly known as *spam*. It imposes penalties on senders who violate the act by intentionally falsifying their identities or the content of their messages to consumers. The act requires all unsolicited marketing email to have a valid return email address so recipients can easily ask to be removed from mass email lists.

Even though this CAN-SPAM Act is in effect, unsolicited email is still rampant and it is still difficult to get off unsolicited email lists. Unfortunately, spam is here to stay; the best hope is to minimize it as much as possible.

Here are some options to help minimize spam email:

- **Manage spam**—The Federal Trade Commission has developed an entire website on managing spam email at www.ftc.gov/bcp/conline/edcams/spam/index.html.

- **Opt out of unsolicited email**—The Direct Marketing Association has an Email Preference Service to help you reduce unsolicited commercial emails. To opt out of receiving unsolicited commercial email, use the online form at www.dmaconsumers.org/offemaillist.html. Your online request is effective for one year.

- **Give out a separate email address to certain organizations or Internet sites**—Keep your primary email address for friends and business associates. In some cases, you can't view an Internet site without giving your email address to log in. To avoid unsolicited email from these sites, you could set up and use a free email account with Hotmail (www.hotmail.com) or Yahoo (www.yahoo.com) and give that address to these types of sites.

- **Purchase third-party software that filters your email for spam before downloading**—Such programs include SafetyBar (www.cloudmark.com), Norton AntiSpam (www.norton.com), SpamKiller (www.mcafee.com), and Qurb (www.qurb.com). Or visit www.removeyou.com, which lists other anti-spam software.

- **Activate your email software or ISP system to scan automatically for junk or spam email**—Usually this option is under the Rules or Filters function.

- **Send a copy of the spam email to the Federal Trade Commission at spam@uce.gov**—They do investigate the sender and the email and sometimes bring legal action against noncompliant entities.

Managing Incoming Email

Adopt the idea that your email inbox is like the inbox on your desk: a place that information should come into and move out of quickly. Your goal is to maintain an empty inbox. As I mentioned, only email that you haven't yet read or still must take action on should remain in your inbox. All other email should ideally be removed from your inbox so you can easily view those emails that need action or response. This approach keeps your inbox current and highlights the items you must take action on.

Here are the steps to take to manage the incoming email:

1. **Eliminate unnecessary email.** After your incoming email has been downloaded, scan your email and delete all the unnecessary email, such as spam, updates, newsletters, and other email you do not need to read or respond to. Get rid of what you don't need, right away!

2. **Determine priorites and respond.** After you have scanned and deleted frivolous email, begin by responding to the high-priority emails first. The priority emails are the ones that require an immediate response based on the sender or content or are directly related to current projects, initiatives, and action items you are working on. You can sort the incoming email by sender if you prefer to respond to certain individuals first. Click the From in the header to quickly sort by name. Or you can sort by date, if that is easier, by clicking Received in the header. Then, respond to the remaining email, including personal messages, newsletters, and forwarded email after your high-priority emails have been completed.

   If you're uncertain what to do with a specific email message, begin by asking yourself, "Is there any action that I need to take?" If so, take action and respond appropriately. If the message requires no action on your part, ask yourself, "Is it important information to save?" If so, file it appropriately. Lastly, ask yourself, "Is it information that someone else needs?" If so, forward the email to the appropriate person. If you have answered *no* to all the questions, you most likely can delete the email.

3. **File or delete email.** If you follow the three *R*s of email outlined earlier, you will respond to most messages immediately after you've read them and then delete or file the original email message thereafter. Emails that are quick responses or reminders most likely do not need to be kept and can be deleted.

> **tip** If you experience a high volume of CC and BCC email, consider whether this is email you need to be receiving. If not, let the sender know. Often, the sender CC's or BCC's people because she's unsure of what others (usually managers or supervisors) want to see. Communicate to your staff and colleagues which distribution lists you would like to be on or off. This helps reduce the number of email you receive via CC and BCC.

Other emails are important correspondence and should be filed and kept for reference. File those email messages in the email file folders you have created. Be sure to save attachments separately to your hard drive before you file the email in a folder. Emails that contain contact information, websites, resources, future action items, or an event or calendar item should be immediately moved or copied to the appropriate location of that particular information. Information you don't immediately file in its proper folder is likely to become lost. You will save time, frustration, and the inconvenience of tracking down hard-to-locate information if you take the time to immediately file your messages.

Consolidating Multiple Email Accounts

If you have multiple email accounts, such as one for business and one for personal messages, you might want to manage all accounts with one email program. Managing all email accounts with a single program is easier than using multiple programs to manage multiple accounts.

You can choose to have all your email accounts directed into your software's primary inbox; do this by setting up additional email accounts in your software. In Outlook, you can set up these accounts by choosing Tools, Email Accounts, Add a New Email Account, and filling in the appropriate account information. Alternatively, you can create separate inbox file folders in your email software system and direct separate email addresses to download directly into those designated folders.

After you have added the new email accounts, you have to create new email file folders for the separate account inboxes and then create a rule or filter to direct the incoming email from a particular email address into a designated file folder. If you choose to have different email addresses move directly into separate inbox file folders, you have to be diligent about checking them daily to ensure you don't miss any important email.

If you have email downloaded into a handheld, such as the BlackBerry or Treo, you need to determine the best method to manage emails from two locations. The best option is to have your handheld configured so that downloaded emails and email files sync between your desktop and handheld. This way, you can download email into your handheld and delete or file email and the new email will sync with your computer when you return to the office. This eliminates the need to manage the same email twice—once on your handheld and once on your desktop.

If your particular handheld does not sync with your email manager, you can have the email saved on the server when it downloads onto your handheld. This way, when you get back to your office, your email downloads into your email software so it can be saved, filed, and backed up. This feature usually is an option on your handheld that you choose during configuration to set up the email account.

Avoid Printing!

Avoid the paper pileup and refrain from printing emails unless absolutely necessary. Many people print emails so they can have a hardcopy reminder to go back and answer or otherwise deal with the message contents, but printing and managing unnecessary hard copies of email messages can be a big timewaster. Again, save yourself time and headaches and deal with messages as soon as you read them, rather than printing and filing them for later action.

 Your brain can trick you into thinking you have completed the email action when you have only printed it and deleted the electronic message from your inbox. Until you've responded to and deleted or filed the message, however, you haven't handled the email. It is better to keep action-related email in your email inbox.

Sometimes you do need to print email for various reasons, such as when you are preparing for a meeting and need to print directions, an agenda, and other handouts. Print the email and, when you are done with the paper printouts, recycle them. If you need to keep the email message, save the email in the appropriate file folder for retrieval and access in the future. This saves the hassle of trying to file paper of all the emails you print. If you determine that you want to keep an email in paper form, file it immediately in the appropriate paper file category.

Many people find printed email easier to read than onscreen messages. If you are among this group, be diligent and address the email right away after you print and read it. After you have responded, recycle the paper. Also, consider changing the font size on your email program to read emails on your computer screen. In Microsoft Outlook, you can increase the font size of the text in an email, which makes it easier to read. Open an email and then select View, Text Size, Largest and the email text automatically increases for viewing purposes, as shown in Figure 7.4. When you reply to an email, it automatically returns to the original text size.

FIGURE 7.4

Shown here in Microsoft Outlook, you can increase the size of the text to read emails more easily. Select View, Text Size, Largest. The email text automatically increases in size. When you reply to an email, it returns to its original text format.

To do list

- ☐ Create an email file system that parallels your master outline.
- ☐ Create email folders and subfolders.
- ☐ Save messages as text files.
- ☐ Save email attachments to the hard drive to ensure retrieval later.
- ☐ Learn to archive email and set up an automatic archiving schedule.

Building the File System

Another key to successful email management is to have a file folder system developed to store and file incoming email. After you have responded and taken action on an email, you either delete or file it. As you've learned in this chapter, you manage email effectively by creating the file habit.

Things You'll Need

- ☐ Email software
- ☐ Master filing outline created in Chapter 3

Creating an Email File Structure

Return to the master outline structure you created in Chapter 3, "Joining the Electronic Age of Organizing," and create a similar file structure in your email program. Create a parallel email file system with your paper and electronic file structures. Having similar file systems will help you remember where your information is located.

There will be slight differences between these two file structures. For instance, you might need a Travel email file folder to store your travel itineraries and hotel/car confirmations, but you might not need a Travel file for your electronic documents. Customize your email file structure as you need to with the information you receive.

Be wary of creating too many additional folders that leave too many options to choose from—ideally, you should not have to scroll down more than a page length to see all your email folders. If you do have a long list of email file folders, consider subfiling under other primary topics.

As suggested earlier, it can be helpful to create action-related email folders such as Follow-up, Action, or Pending. The key is to ensure that you check these email folders daily or weekly to make sure emails are being handled and not forgotten. If you find you aren't habitually checking these folders, go back to the standard system of keeping all action-related email in your inbox. To organize these action folders in the top of the line of your email folder structure, add an underscore (_) or the letter *a* in front of the name of the file folder—for example, _Action.

Creating Folders

All email programs have the capability to create email file folders and subfolders. It is best to create individual email file folders in your inbox, as shown in Figure 7.5. After you have read and responded to an email, merely drag the email message from the inbox into the appropriate email file folder. You can create subfolders as well under primary folders. In Microsoft Outlook, highlight the folder in which you want to create subfiles and select File, New, Folder.

FIGURE 7.5

Shown here in Microsoft Outlook is a sample email file outline structure. To create a new file folder, highlight the inbox and select File, New, Folder; the New Folder window appears. Enter the name of the file folder and click OK.

If you need to archive email from multiple years, consider creating topic subfolders for each year, as shown in Figure 7.6. Then, file email from the current year in the new file structure. This organization saves you much time when trying to locate a specific email from any year.

Saving Emails in Other Forms

You can also save email messages directly into the My Documents folders on your hard or shared drive. Then, you have to manage only one electronic file structure on your hard drive. This arrangement also allows you to delete emails more frequently or set up auto delete.

If you want to save an email to your hard drive, you should save it as a text file (**.txt**). Text files usually are easier to open and don't rely on email software; text files also have more protection from changes due to system upgrades and can therefore be easier to open and access in the future. You can save emails as text files in most email software programs. To perform this save in .txt format, follow these steps:

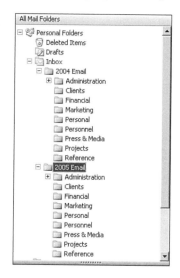

FIGURE 7.6

In this example (shown in Microsoft Outlook), folders have been created to hold email for 2004 and 2005.

1. Open the email, go to the upper toolbar, and select File, Save As. The Save As window opens.

2. At the bottom of the Save As window in the File Type field, select the .txt option.

3. The filename defaults to be the email subject line. Consider changing the filename to be more descriptive and adding the sender's name before saving.

4. Select Save.

Saving Attachments

Attachments are not technically saved within an email file. Email attachments are usually downloaded to a separate file folder in your hard drive or on the network drive. Attachments are therefore not a part of an email program but rather are links embedded in an email. With Microsoft Outlook in particular, email attachments are downloaded to a temporary file within your hard drive. This temporary file can be difficult to locate, however. The temporary file also is deleted when system cleanup operations are performed.

If your email attachments are downloaded to a separate drive, links to attachments can be broken with system upgrades or when the file is moved to a different drive. If that happens, you might be unable to open or find the original attachment in the future. To protect your attachments, save them in your electronic file structure on your hard drive. This ensures that those attachments are accessible in the future and preserves the integrity of your data and documents. Be sure to check the filename before saving to make any necessary changes.

Archiving Emails

Email files can get very large, and often email network servers slow down and lose performance because of the volume of email files. Most IT departments ask users to either delete or archive email to reduce the size of the email file. Some companies automatically delete email after a certain time period (60–90 days) if it is not archived. With personal computer systems, when email files get too large, the software can lose speed and performance. This generally happens when the file size gets larger than 250,000KB. If you usually don't keep email, you probably don't have to worry about archiving. If you have a tendency to keep most of your email, you probably need to set up a regular system to archive older email to maintain performance with your system and ensure the safekeeping of your data.

Most email programs have the capability to archive email. When you archive email, you create a separate window and file from your primary inbox structure. Usually, this archive file is saved on a hard drive separate from the email file on your network server. That archiving window or file holds all the messages that are older than a specified date. In most email programs you must activate the archive feature for it to automatically archive emails. Setting up an archive usually solves the problem of your current inbox being at capacity with most networked server systems. It also helps to reduce the file size so your primary inbox functions more quickly.

If you are on a networked system, consult with your IT department before setting up an archive yourself. If you have a standalone system, you can usually configure your archive yourself following the Help directions in your email software. If you are not sure whether your email program has an archive feature, consult the Help query or your IT department or consultant.

Microsoft Outlook has a function called Auto Archive, which creates a separate archive email file from your primary Outlook file. When you open Outlook, you can access this archive file system by clicking in the folder (once activated) named Archive Folders. When you set up Auto Archive, it automatically moves emails within their folders to the archive file after a certain date, which you can determine. Then, you can just open your archive to view old emails.

To activate the archive in Microsoft Outlook, select Tools, Options and click the Other tab. Then click AutoArchive (as shown in Figure 7.7), which opens the AutoArchive window, where you can choose options for archiving. The Run Auto Archive options needs to be checked initially to open the window options.

Instead of archiving your entire file system, you can choose to archive only certain file folders. This is handy if you want to perform different archiving functions with each file folder. For instance, for certain folders, you may want to delete all folder contents after six months and not archive the older email. This regular clean-up process will also free up space on a regular basis so that you don't receive the inbox full messages from your IT department.

FIGURE 7.7

Shown here in Microsoft Outlook, the Options window is used to activate the AutoArchive function. Click the AutoArchive button to select options and create the archive file.

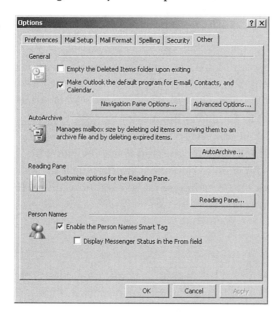

To set up auto archive for each file folder in Microsoft Outlook, right-click the email folder and select Properties. Click the AutoArchive tab, as shown in Figure 7.8. Select Archive This Folder Using These Settings (the third option), and then select options as desired.

FIGURE 7.8

In Microsoft Outlook, use a folder's Properties window to set up archive options for that specific email folder.

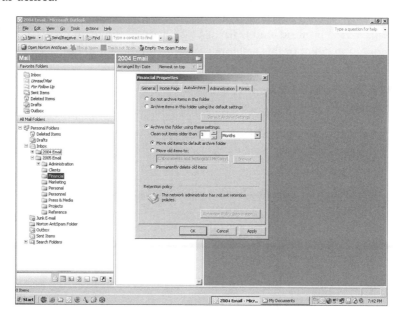

You can also create your own archiving method within your current email file structure. You might want to create a new file folder system for each calendar or fiscal year and archive the prior year in a separate file folder named for that year, as shown previously in Figure 7.6.

With Microsoft Entourage for Mac users, you can click and drag an entire email file folder to the Mac desktop. This automatically creates a copy of the email file folder and gives the file an extension of **.mbox**. You can then put this

note It is recommended you keep emails for at least two years for legal purposes. Depending on your industry and company policies, you might be required to keep emails longer than two years. When you organize your emails by year, it makes retrieving and purging them in the future easier.

.mbox file in your electronic file structure and delete the email file folder from the Entourage program. If you want to retrieve the **.mbox** file later, merely click and drag the **.mbox** file back into Entourage and you will have immediate access to the file folder and the email contents.

Summary

Managing email can be one of the most time-consuming aspects of your work day. To reduce that time and manage email efficiently, consider setting up a regular schedule for checking and responding to email—for example, no more than three times a day. Take time to manage email completely by applying the three *Rs* rule of read, respond, and remove. Consider keeping in your inbox only emails that you have not read, need to respond to, or need to take action on. All other emails should either be deleted or be moved to a file folder. The ultimate goal is to create an empty in-box. Set up an email file folder system that mimics your paper and electronic systems. Avoid printing emails when possible and keep them archived electronically. By managing email in this fashion, you will save time and not be overwhelmed with the daily email communications.

Here are the key things to remember when managing email:

- Only have items you haven't responded to or read in your inbox.
- Don't delay the decision. Read, respond, and remove email at one time.
- Create an email file structure that parallels your paper and electronic file structures.
- Determine your best times to respond to and manage email.
- Set up an automatic archiving system for outdated email.
- Avoid printing your emails, if possible.

In the next chapter, "Managing Projects Effectively," we discuss the project cycle and how to create a project plan. Delegation techniques are also discussed. With many options of project-management tools, you learn which ones might be right for your type of projects.

Managing Projects Effectively

8

In today's business world, almost everyone has projects to manage. Whether you are an administrative assistant or a CEO, project management is part of your job. And, from the annual holiday party to a company relocation or the implementation of new strategic initiatives, each project needs management and planning. Our business culture is one of change and continuous improvement. Individuals who can effectively implement projects are becoming more and more in demand in the workplace. Even in the hit show *The Apprentice*, the participants are rated on their project management skills, including management, communication, delegation, and effective project planning.

The definition of a project is simply a "planned undertaking." Projects can be large or small, but the key to any successful project is effective planning. The initial planning you do with all projects will save you time in the future. All projects have various components in which each aspect should be addressed and defined before taking action. This helps to ensure that your project stays on track and you plan for any challenges or obstacles that might come your way.

It is important with all projects to learn how to break down the project into manageable action steps and integrate it into your day or workweek. Doing this keeps the project moving forward and avoids procrastination. In this chapter, we take you through a step-by-step process of how to develop a project plan and break down any project into manageable steps.

You also learn about the many options for organizing projects, both on paper and electronically. You can use project management software such as Microsoft Project or even spreadsheet programs such as Excel to track and plan projects. You also can organize projects in your electronic or paper time-management tool or software. In this chapter, you learn various ways to track and organize projects of many types.

Projects usually entail teamwork and good communication. Regular project meetings are therefore necessary to anticipate problems and to provide updates. After action items have been assigned or delegated, the project manager needs to follow up with team members to track their progress and encourage accountability. In this chapter, you learn how to effectively delegate project responsibilities and follow up on their progress.

To do list

- ☐ Determine the objective and purpose of the project.
- ☐ List all the action steps needed to complete the task.
- ☐ Estimate the time and determine due dates with each task.
- ☐ Develop a budget and estimate costs.
- ☐ Assign tasks to specific individuals.

Defining and Developing the Project Plan

Whether your project is large or small, it is important to define and consider all aspects of it before beginning. Understanding how you will approach the project helps you organize and implement the project more effectively. If you can master the project planning process, it doesn't matter what type or size of project you have; the same methods will apply.

Projects take longer and are more time-consuming if you skip the project planning phase. Some project teams jump right into the implementation stage without planning beforehand. This inevitably makes the project take longer and causes more wasted time through lack of proper focus, guidelines, and structure. In this section, you learn how to structure and plan your project effectively, so you know exactly what must be done, when it must be done, what will be required to complete the project, and who will complete each step.

Things You'll Need

- ❑ Paper and pen or pencil
- ❑ Computer software tools such as Microsoft Word, Excel, or Project
- ❑ Notebooks, file folders, hanging folders, magazine boxes, and labels
- ❑ Project forms, spiral notebooks, or project planning day planner pages

Determining the Objective and Purpose

Before beginning any project, you and your project members need to determine the objective and purpose of it. This often is the most overlooked and disregarded aspect of project management. Knowing the purpose and goal helps you, and others, make appropriate decisions and choices during planning and implementation. Clarifying priorities and aligning team members help keep projects focused and on task. A lack of understanding of the ultimate purpose of the project can hinder and delay decision-making, and it can lead to failed projects. Take the time to think through the objective and purpose of each and every project. If you have done the project before, review the lessons you learned that you would want to incorporate into goals for the upcoming project. If management delegated this project to you, clarify their expectations and objectives of the project. Discuss or consider these questions to help determine the objective and purpose of your project:

- What is the ultimate goal of the project?
- Which objectives will be met if the project is successful?
- Of those objectives, which one is the most important? Why?
- What expectations does management have of this project?
- What lessons have been learned from similar prior projects?

When you've answered the questions, use your answers to develop a consolidated bulleted list of goals. To illustrate developing a project plan, let's use an example of planning a company-wide annual meeting of 100 people that will be held in mid-December. Here are the goals for this sample project:

- To communicate to employees the strategic plan for the coming year (most important)
- To build colleague rapport and enforce the company's mission and values
- To reach 90% of attendance with all staff members
- To have an enjoyable and fun event

Listing All the Action Steps

After the objective is determined, create a separate task list detailing all the action steps required to accomplish the project. Projects don't get done in one giant step but through multiple baby steps. Breaking down the tasks can be done formally or informally through a variety of methods, such as facilitated meetings, brainstorming sessions, mind-mapping, or freehand writing. Whichever method you choose, you should have a complete list of every action step needed to complete the project.

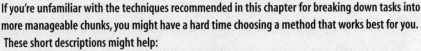

TECHNIQUES FOR BREAKING DOWN TASKS

If you're unfamiliar with the techniques recommended in this chapter for breaking down tasks into more manageable chunks, you might have a hard time choosing a method that works best for you. These short descriptions might help:

- **Facilitated meetings**—A *facilitated meeting* is a guided meeting lead by a neutral person (generally not a group participant or leader). The facilitator helps manage group processes and dynamics to ensure that a meeting is well-run, remains focused, and addresses essential issues and topics. Facilitated meetings work well for large projects.

- **Brainstorming sessions**—The act of *brainstorming* involves focusing on one particular topic or problem and thinking through all the possible ideas or solutions. Brainstorming is designed to determine the best approach, no matter how unconventional, radical, or improbable it seems. When brainstorming is in process, someone in the group should record all the ideas on a tablet or easel. At the end of the session, the group reviews and organizes the ideas into groups and a timeline. For more detailed information about how to do brainstorming, visit the Mind Tools website at www.mindtools.com/brainstm.html.

- **Mind-Mapping**—*Mind-mapping* is a technique used to unleash ideas from the brain. Mind-mapping starts with writing a topical word or phrase on a sheet of paper. From that word, you draw lines out and write additional words, pictures, or graphics that relate to subheadings or topics from that word. Then, from those words or graphics, you draw additional lines. For more information about mind-mapping, visit the websites of the originators of the technique—Tony Buzan (www.mind-map.com) and Peter Russell (www.peterussell.com).

- **Freehand writing**—*Freehand writing* is a conventional way in which to write down ideas on a piece of paper. You write down the topic at the top of the paper and list bulleted words or phrases that relate to that topic. Your mind might come up with ideas in a logical sequence or not. With project planning, write down all the action items in a list view. When you complete the freehand list, you can organize it into categories, a timeline, and a priority structure.

You will find in the initial breakdown process that large tasks are identified as major components of the project. After the major components are identified, break those down even further into smaller tasks. Depending on the size of the project, you might have to break down tasks into even smaller tasks. Ideally, you should have the project broken down so that each task takes less than 4 hours to complete (this is merely a guideline, of course).

You will edit, add to, and delete from the task list throughout the life of the project. However, it is important at this stage just to write all the foreseeable action steps you need to complete and break them down into manageable steps.

Don't forget to consider the final action steps necessary to wrap up a project after the main tasks are completed. These final action items could include

- Writing the final report
- Sending thank-you notes
- Processing bills and invoices
- Developing the final financial report
- Providing training to staff or colleagues to maintain the project
- Evaluating or discussing the lessons learned
- Writing or discussing the project performance with team members

These action items are easy to overlook and leave out of the original plan, and project staff can find themselves scrambling to complete them at the last minute. Don't forget to add these wrap-up tasks to your project plan so they are not forgotten.

Estimating Time and Due Dates

Determining time and due dates for each action step establishes the sequence in which tasks should be completed. Begin by determining an exact (or optimal) due date for when the entire project should be completed. In the case of our example, the annual company meeting is to be held December 15. Then, estimate the approximate or optimal deadline date for each action item within the overall project time-frame. This backward planning approach allows you to know before you start the project how much time you will need to allocate each week or day to complete it.

Then, assign an approximate amount of time that each action item will take. For example, if you need to develop handouts for the meeting, how long should this take you or someone else in the project team? In our example, we have estimated approximately one 8-hour day to develop handouts. This is only an approximation and can, or will, change as we proceed in the project. If you find, as in our example in Figure 8.1, that some action items will take longer than 4 hours, consider breaking them down even further, if possible. Add up the time needed and figure a total time needed each week to get the project completed on time.

Determine the priority level of each action step if you have a medium to large project. Clarifying priorities helps you know which tasks to address first when you are under tight deadlines and have limited time in the week. When you realize that you have limited resources and money, you can then address those actions that are critical versus merely optional. You can prioritize using the A,B,C or 1,2,3 coding system. Tasks prioritized as A or 1, for example, might be essential to the project's success, tasks labeled C or 3 might be relatively inconsequential, and the B or 2-level tasks might be helpful elements of the overall project that should be completed if possible.

caution Build in "margin" time for each project. Every project involves certain unplanned-for tasks, such as documentation review, an approval process, revisions/corrections, or the inevitable crises that occur. So, remember to build in extra time for tasks that need review or approval. Also, use your experience from similar projects to build in time for dealing with contingencies and unpredictable scenarios that might crop up during the course of your project.

Estimating the Budget

To determine the budget for your project, you need to assign expenses to each applicable task in your task-list breakdown. Be sure to add in a cushion for hidden or unknown costs, such as cost estimates you have not received, mistakes or errors in quantity or amount ordered, or additional resources needed but not known at the time. You can either increase each line item by a certain amount or percentage (10%–15% is usually adequate) or add one total contingency amount line at the bottom for unknown expenses. Although you want the budget to be as detailed as possible, remember that it is merely an estimate of expenses to help you plan. If you are working with a mandated budget, you need to work backward from the total budget amount to ensure your action items meet your budget requirements.

For smaller projects, I recommend that you integrate the budget into the project plan; for medium to large projects, I suggest creating a separate document for budgets. Most project software programs, such as MS Project, have financial functions to help you develop budgets. You can also download Excel budget templates; go to Microsoft Online at www.microsoft.com and then click Templates from the sidebar list.

Here are some categories of costs you'll need to consider when developing your project's budget:

- **Labor**—Approximate cost of each staff person working on the project. This can be estimated by the total hours needed to complete the project and an average hourly staff rate.

- **Vendors**—The cost of consultants, vendors, and suppliers needed. Most vendors supply an estimate of costs to include in your budget.

- **Supplies and materials**—The cost of equipment, supplies, and materials that will need to be purchased such as tools, technology, and other miscellaneous items.

- **Marketing and promotion**—All costs associated with marketing and promoting the project, including advertising, printing, graphic development, and mailing.

- **Profit and gain**—Some projects require a profit or financial gain to be successful. This is especially true with donations given at fundraisers or silent auctions where there is not a set price or fee determined. This is usually an income line item based on projected profit. For example, if you are planning a fundraising event and expect 200 people to attend and give an average donation of $20, you would add $4,000 into the profit and gain line item.

- **Revenue**—Some projects procure revenue, such as events, parties, and fundraisers based on a set fee or cost for the project or event. Estimate the amount of revenue income based on projected attendance multiplied by the fee or cost.

Assigning Responsibility

Within project teams, it is important that each task be assigned to specific team members. In addition to team members, external vendors and consultants can be responsible for completing individual tasks. However, usually within a project team there is a designated point of contact for each vendor or consultant to oversee that the designated task is monitored and completed by the vendor or consultant. Tracking the person(s) responsible and points of contact helps you monitor and follow up with individuals or vendors as necessary. Assigning a responsible team member helps create accountability for each task within the project and helps ensure that all tasks are completed as scheduled.

Tracking Notes and Comments

During the course of project planning, there will be notes—comments you will want to track with each action item to provide additional information, guidance, or suggestions. I suggest you create a column or text area in your project plan to track this type of information, as shown in Figure 8.1. These notes could include the following types of information:

- Internet sites to get additional information or find resources
- Individuals who are not members of the project team but who might be additional resources

- Guidelines and restrictions to decisions
- Other resources that might be helpful to complete a task, such as files, documents, software, and so on

FIGURE 8.1

A Microsoft Excel example of a complete project plan using a spreadsheet format.

	A	B	C	D	E	F	G
1	Project Name: Annual Company Meeting	Date: December 15th	Purpose: To communicate to employees the strategic plan for the coming year				
2	Task	Due Date	Approx Time	Budget	Person Assigned	Resources	Notes/ Updates
3	Find Location of Meeting	September 15th	2-3 days	$1,000	Kathy	Contact Stephanie who planned last year's meeting	
4	* Visit possible facilities	August 15th					
5	* Approve contract with Accounting Director	August 30th					
6	Find Keynote Speaker	October 1st	1-2 days	$1,500	Jim		
7	* Request Speaker Information					Use the local speaker's bureau for options	
8	* Write thank you note concluding event	December 16th					
9	Determine food or drink	November 15th	2 hours	$1,500	Kathy	Call Jane and find out cateror used for their company's annual meeting	
10	Develop Invitation and RSVP Process	October 15th	4 hours	$0	Mary	Use template and database from last year on H drive	
11	Develop Agenda and Program	November 1st	4-5 hours	$0	Project Team	Plan meeting with management to determine agenda and program	
12	* Meeting with management to determine initial agenda	October 1st					
13	* Practise run through of meeting with all persons on agenda	October 20th					
14	Determine AV Needs	November 15th	1-2 hours	$600	Kathy	Use Internet to find local AV rental company	
15	Develop and Print Handouts and Company Materials	December 1st	1 day	$150	Mary	Consult Marketing Dept to help with formatting. Use intern to copy materials	
16			Total Time Needed: 7.5 days	Total Budget: $4750			

PROJECT MANAGEMENT RESOURCES

The following are some project management websites that provide useful resources to plan and implement projects:

- **Columbia University (http://www.columbia.edu/~jm2217/#RecReading)**—Columbia University has an extensive list of project management resources that include sample project templates, samples, guidelines, and links to other project-related websites.

- **PM Forum (www.pmforum.org)**—This site provides international information on project management resources.

- **Project Magazine (www.projectmagazine.com)**—This online site has some good, short articles on managing projects.

- **Project Management Institute (www.pmi.org)**—The group that hosts this site is the association for project management professionals. They offer training, workshops, and certification for project management.

To do list

- ☐ Create a project plan in project management software or in spreadsheet or table format.
- ☐ Assign responsibility for plan updates.
- ☐ Determine a distribution list for the plan.
- ☐ Purchase customized project forms or templates if you prefer to handwrite the project plan.

Creating a Project Plan

So far, this chapter has discussed the benefits of developing a project plan. Now that you know the components of that plan, it's time to learn how to create the actual plan, in either electronic or hard-copy form.

Your project plan or map helps you and everyone on the project team stay on track. You will view the project plan weekly and integrate the upcoming action items into your calendar and task list. And, you can distribute the project plan to all team members and external parties who'll be participating in project tasks, including vendors, other colleagues, and management. That way, everyone who is interested in or has a stake in the outcome can track the project's progress. Remember to assign responsibility for updating the plan to someone on the project team. Updates could be the responsibility of one person or all team members, but the responsibility must be formally assigned to ensure that the project plan is updated regularly.

Things You'll Need

- ☐ Project management software
- ☐ Computer/handheld device
- ☐ Paper planning tool, if appropriate

Using Project Management Software

For larger projects, you might want to consider creating the project plan within formal project management software, such as Microsoft Project, as shown in Figure 8.2. Most project management programs provide standard fields for tracking all the necessary information and tasks within the project. They also provide excellent timelines, charts, and graphs to help you graphically illustrate the project's plan and progress. If you make adjustments to due dates, the software usually adjusts future tasks accordingly. I recommend that you use project management software for projects that involve more than six people and that will take more than 4–5 months to complete.

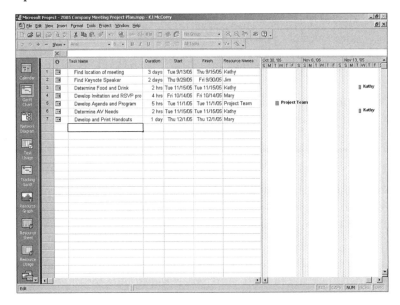

You don't have to use sophisticated project management software to plan projects. Some teams purchase project software and never use it because no one on the team has time to learn how to use the software. Don't let this be a barrier to planning your project and creating an electronic project plan. You can use a simple Excel spreadsheet or Word table for creating your project plan. Both formats are easy to email as attachments and don't require the installation of special software. You can use Microsoft standard project planning templates located online or create your own. If you create your own project table, create the following headings: Task, Due Date, Approximate Time, Budget, Person Assigned, Resources, and Notes/Comments, as shown previously in Figure 8.1.

You can also use the contact management (CM) or personal information management (PIM) software, such as Outlook, Lotus Notes, or GroupWise, to create your project management plan. With networked CM and PIM tools, you can create public or shared electronic task lists in the CM or PIM that can be viewed by everyone internally in your company. Usually you need your IT consultant to set up the shared task list. This saves the hassle

tip For Mac users, Entourage software has a project management tool that provides a separate task list and the capability to link key emails and documents into one view. This enables users to see all the information related to that project in a single view. The latest version of Lotus Notes also has a built-in project management tool called TeamRoom, which is an information sharing, tracking, and communication tool that is excellent for teams that are dispersed geographically and not in one location.

of sending an updated version of document files to project team members each time an update is made. It also alleviates the need to learn a new project software. The other advantage of using existing company CM or PIM software is that tasks can be copied into your personal electronic task list or calendar, eliminating the need to reenter data.

Creating a Hard-Copy Project Plan

If you are the only one involved in your project and you prefer handwriting your project plan, purchase graph paper or spiral bound project planners (manufactured by Tops Docket and Mead) that can help you write the plan in spreadsheet format. Some day planners also have separate note or graph pages designed for project planning. Or print a project template available online and handwrite the information. You can download an array of project forms from Project Connections (www.projectconnections.com) after you subscribe to the service (the first 15 days are free). Microsoft also has Excel to-do lists for project templates available for download free from its website at www.microsoft.com.

In addition, wall calendars and planners can be used as project planners. These are useful if you want to have a visual reminder of your project in a conference room, a hallway, or an office. At-A-Glance (www.ataglance.com) manufactures a variety of undated eraseable wall planners and calendars that could be used for project planning.

caution One of the challenges with tracking handwritten project plans is that project plan information is continually changing; therefore, changing and updating handwritten project plans is more difficult and time-consuming. If you decide to use a handwritten project plan, be diligent about updating it periodically; otherwise, it will become too outdated for you to use or plan from.

PROJECT MANAGEMENT SOFTWARE

The following are some project management software packages that can help you plan, manage, and track projects:

- **FastTrack Schedule (www.aecsoft.com)**—FastTrack Schedule works with both PC and Mac systems. It also has the capability to synchronize with Palm OS handheld systems. This is handy if you need to have your project plan with you outside the office. This is a good, easy-to-use software for medium to small projects.

- **Microsoft Project (http://office.microsoft.com/en-us/FX010857951033.aspx)**—Microsoft Project is a good project management tool for large, complex projects that have multiple people and resources involved. The newer version of the software is on the higher price end.

- **Milestones (www.kidasa.com)**—Milestones sets itself apart from the other project management applications by its use and design of graphics within each window view. It creates beautiful illustrations of the project plan, schedule, and resources in a clear visual manner for presentations.
- **Project KickStart (www.projectkickstart.com)**—Project KickStart is good project management tool for medium to small projects. The software links with Microsoft Word, Excel, PowerPoint, and Project for the easy importing of data. It also links with most major project software.

To do list

- ☐ Integrate your project tasks into your calendar and/or task list.
- ☐ Schedule regular project meetings.
- ☐ Monitor the project by planning follow-up calls or emails to other colleagues and project team members.
- ☐ Delegate effectively by providing all the necessary information to complete the task.
- ☐ Create a project file in your paper, electronic, and email file structures.
- ☐ Determine the best method (file folder, notebook, day planner, or magazine box) for organizing your paper documentation.

Implementing the Project

Review the project plan weekly and integrate your designated action items into your own calendar and/or task list. Remember to check daily for those tasks you must complete and to allow yourself adequate time. If the task takes considerable time, thought, and development, consider planning it in the morning. If a task takes longer than 2–4 hours to complete, consider breaking it down into smaller action items you can accomplish throughout the day. If the task can't be broken down, block out adequate time in your calendar for completing it and treat that time commitment just as you would that for a very important meeting. Remember to mark the task as "done" when you finish.

When you begin major action items for the project, stay on task until your task is completed. This allows you to stay focused, so you can move quickly onto the next task. Consider clearing your desk before you begin, so other documents and action items don't distract you. Don't overwhelm yourself by worrying about all the tasks that need to get done. Remember to do one task at a time—each baby step leads you closer to the project's completion.

Things You'll Need

- ❏ Your project plan
- ❏ Filing folders, binders, expandable files, file boxes, and other filing materials, as appropriate
- ❏ Task manager/calendar

Monitoring and Follow-up

Communication is key to any successful team project. The project manager or coordinator should monitor the project plan and follow up with the person responsible for each action item either on or just after due dates. Performing regular task follow-up is key to maintaining accountability for all individuals involved with the project. Projects often fail or become delayed because of a lack of follow-up or monitoring.

The project manager or coordinator should schedule follow-up calls or emails in her task-tracking tool. By scheduling the follow-up in your calendar, you're more likely to keep on top of the project. If you are using your electronic task tool, use the notes section to track the follow-up actions you have taken with others. Note the date and time of the follow-up, whether you called or emailed, the status of that task, and the project completion date. Tracking this data helps you in the future, in case you need to follow up with that task again. And recording this information lets you forget it and move on, so you can concentrate on other tasks.

Schedule regular project meetings either weekly or monthly. Regular project meetings help identify problems and provide necessary updates for others. During these meetings, you have an opportunity to uncover developing problems and determine the appropriate corrective actions. All members should come prepared to update the team on the status of their action items. The project plan itself should be updated to reflect any changes in deadline dates or additional action items. In Chapter 9, "Maximizing Meeting Time," we discuss in more detail how to have effective meetings.

tip If the project begins to fall behind schedule, take immediate action. Consider renegotiating deadline dates, requesting more resources, or deleting your lower-priority action items. Taking corrective action when you first notice that a problem is developing helps the project stay on track.

Delegating Effectively

Some tasks involve delegating responsibilities to others who are not part of the project team, such as an administrative assistant, an intern, other department personnel, or temporary help. These individuals won't have as much information and background on the project, so you will need to provide complete instructions, guidelines, and parameters for the roles you are delegating to them. Poor delegation leads to incomplete or failed tasks—problems which more often than not could have been avoided with proper communication. Here are some guidelines for effective delegation:

- **Review the overall objective and purpose**—This gives the delegatee essential data to help implement the task and avoid procrastination and indecision resulting from lack of data.

- **Establish deadline dates**—Be clear about when you need the action item completed. Negotiate due dates as needed.

- **Provide clear and concise guidelines**—If there is a certain method in which the task needs to be completed, describe the method clearly. If the delegatee can determine the best way for completing the task, make sure you've communicated any important parameters.

- **Give additional resources**—Let the delegatee know whether there are additional resources that might be helpful in completing the task or in finding answers to questions or issues that arise. These resources could be other colleagues, websites, or paper or electronic files.

- **Determine follow-up and reporting**—Agree on the communication method (email or phone) and time intervals (daily, weekly, monthly) to follow up or provide updates on the task. This encourages the delegatee to be proactive with the follow-up and increases accountability with the task.

caution Don't delegate something just because you want it off your list. Think about whether it is truly worth anyone's time before you delegate any task. Then, make sure you are really giving it to the appropriate person who has the skills to complete it successfully. Poor delegation, done for the wrong reasons, can leave others feeling resentful and undervalued.

tip Assume positive intent with your fellow project team members. In today's busy world, action items or response to communications can be delayed. Refrain from getting angry and assuming the worst about your colleagues because of lack of follow-through. Assume initially that your team members have the intention to complete the task. Find out what obstacles they are facing and help them work through a plan of action to address those challenges. This ensures good communication and builds teamwork.

Managing the Documentation

There will always be supplementary documentation, financials, correspondence, and meeting notes you need to track with all projects. It is important to create similar project files in your paper, electronic, and email file systems. Consider how you want to subcategorize your project. One way is to break it down either by topic or chronologically. Parallel all your information systems so you have similar subcategories developed in each area, as discussed in Chapter 3, "Joining the Electronic Age of Organizing." Here are some suggested subtopics to consider creating for projects:

- **Project Plan or Map**—This subcategory would include all documentation about the initial development of the project, the master project plan, and any other development notes.

- **Project Meeting Minutes and Notes**—This subcategory would include the regular meeting agendas, minutes, and notes. Ideally it is best to keep this in chronological order for quick access.

- **Budget and Financial Reports**—This subcategory would include all the draft and final budgets, periodic financial reporting, and invoices or bills received for the project.

- **Marketing and Promotion Information**—This subcategory includes all marketing, advertising, press releases, flyers, announcements, and any graphic work documentation.

- **Vendor or Consulting Firm Documentation**—If you have hired any vendors or external consulting firms, you might want to create separate subcategories for each vendor. This file would include cost estimates, proposals, contracts, and all deliverable documentation that was received.

- **Large Task Information**—Depending on the project and your role, there might be large tasks that need their own subcategories to manage the incoming data and documentation. You might need only one section for a large task or multiple sections for other large tasks, depending on the project. In our company meeting project example, there might be a separate section just for the program that would include documentation about speakers, agenda, team-building games, and handouts.

The following are some suggestions for various methods of organizing paper documentation for projects. Whichever method you choose, be consistent. If you create multiple areas in which to store project documentation, finding the necessary information can become difficult and time-consuming:

- **Create a hanging file**—You can designate a separate file drawer for one project or have one file drawer for multiple projects. Determine space based on the scope and size of the project. For a large amount of documentation, purchase box-bottom file or hanging folders or expandable pocket file folders (which also come hanging). Consider using color hanging or tabbed files to color-code projects to make the folders easy to see and recognize.

- **Use a three-ring binder notebook**—Three-ring binder notebooks are great tools to use for organizing project documentation. You can use tabs to designate the subcategories. Binders are especially useful if you need to be mobile with all your information at meetings or offsite.

- **Use your paper planner**—If you use a paper planner, set up a separate tab for each project. You can include a paper copy of the project plan as well as track meeting notes in this section.

- **Use desktop or file boxes**—Desktop or file boxes that are made from cardboard or plastic can also be used to store project documentation. This is useful if you would like your project on your desk or bookcase for easy and immediate access. Wilson Jones makes an excellent product, Perma Easy Files, that are cardboard boxes designed to hold tabbed file folders, as shown in Figure 8.3. They can be purchased or ordered through your local supply store or online.

FIGURE 8.3

Shown here is the Wilson Jones Perma Easy File, which can be used to help organize project documentation and files. For more information about this product, visit www.wilsonjones.com.

Summary

Learning how to effectively plan and manage projects helps you complete projects on time and on budget. Whether you are planning small or large projects, implementing a standard approach to planning all your projects guides you toward becoming a successful project manager. All projects require teamwork, and it is important for the entire project team to be accountable and organized to help ensure project success. In this chapter, you learned these guidelines for successful project planning:

- Plan your project before beginning, and determine the goal and purpose.

- Create a project plan and refer to it weekly; integrate upcoming action items into your daily or weekly calendar.

- Be mindful to communicate all guidelines when delegating tasks to other colleagues.

- Be consistent when organizing project documentation in your paper, electronic, and email files.

In the next chapter, "Maximizing Meeting Time," you learn how to have effective meetings. We will discuss the importance of agendas and taking meeting minutes and cover the necessary roles each of us has in meetings.

Maximizing Meeting Time

9

I hear complaints both ways—either there are too many meetings or just not enough meetings. Some sources estimate that executives waste approximately 8 hours each week in poorly led meetings. When you consider the cost of everyone's time during meetings, this can be quite costly. Most people don't like to meet because too many meetings run on too long and accomplish too little. Devoting time to an activity that offers little or no benefit is frustrating and can inhibit employee morale.

But meetings can be an excellent use of time if managed and run appropriately. The key to effective meetings is being clear about what you want to accomplish and conducting and tracking the meeting in an organized manner.

Establishing goals and objectives before planning a meeting takes forethought; however, that time spent planning will save you time and money in producing effective meetings.

In this chapter, you learn how to determine whether a meeting is the best method of communicating about the issue at hand. If you do need to meet, you can use the skills you learn in this chapter to create an agenda, reinforce the purpose of the meeting, and keep the discussion and participants on-track. This chapter also discusses what types of detailed information you should include in your agenda, to help participants come prepared to conduct a productive meeting.

In this chapter:

* Consider alternative ways to communicate to avoid unnecessary meetings
* Learn how to develop an effective meeting agenda
* Understand the roles and responsibilities of each person at a meeting
* Develop effective methods for tracking personal meeting notes and action items

Everyone has a role in a meeting, and it is up to all of us to create successful and effective meetings. Key roles need to be filled in each meeting, regardless of formality or number of members present. Often, participants become mere observers in a poorly run meeting, and team and meeting effectiveness are reduced, if not lost altogether. In this chapter, we discuss the various roles and responsibilities that each of us has in a meeting.

Last, we discuss the practicality of tracking your own meeting notes and action items. Here, you learn not only how to take personal notes during a meeting, but also what to do with that information when the meeting is over.

To do list

- [ ] Consider other alternatives to holding a meeting.
- [ ] Have clarity on the purpose and goal of the meeting before scheduling it.

Why Are You Meeting?

We have all had that moment when we were sitting in a meeting and thought to ourselves, "What am I doing here?" Before planning a meeting, consider whether you really need to have a meeting at all. Meetings can be an excellent opportunity for

- Communicating, updating, and sharing information with others
- Providing opportunities for others to give opinions and comments and reach decisions or consensus
- Identifying tasks and tracking the progress of projects and initiatives
- Creating, developing, and brainstorming new ideas and initiatives

But not all meetings fit the criteria for a productive use of time. Regular reoccurring meetings, in particular, can become a habit rather than a necessary function. To avoid wasting time on unnecessary meetings, always consider whether you could disseminate the information or discuss the topic without calling a meeting. Also, consider how prepared others will be to participate in the meeting. If you anticipate a lack of participant involvement or preparation time, holding the meeting could be a waste of time and money.

Before planning a meeting, take a moment to consider the following alternatives:

note Information that is highly important might warrant a meeting to ensure that everyone is aware of the announcement.

- **Disseminate the information via email**—If you think the information does not need further discussion or more clarification, send it in an email.

- **Have a phone conference instead**—Discussions held over the phone often take less time than when everyone gathers in a face-to-face meeting. Phone meetings also eliminate the need for participants to travel to and from the meeting, and are therefore particularly important alternatives when members are not in the same location.

- **Have a manager make the decision, rather than discussing it in a meeting**—Some meetings are held strictly to make decisions. If appropriate, have a supervisor, manager, or other leader make the decision; then disseminate it to the group through email or other quick communication. This alternative is particularly useful for decisions that are urgent.

caution Be especially careful not to hold meetings to gather opinions about decisions that have already been made.

tip Just because you were invited to a meeting doesn't necessarily mean you need to be there. Know whether your presence is necessary for the appointment or meeting before accepting the invitation. If it's not, respectfully decline the invitation. If you simply need to be aware of the high points, request that any notes or information be sent to you via email to keep you informed. Be cautious with your time and accept only those invitations to meetings you really need to attend.

If a meeting is necessary, be sure that you clearly understand the purpose of the meeting and that you can explain it clearly to others. If you don't understand the purpose of a meeting you've been invited to, ask! It is the right of every participant to know the reason for his presence at meetings.

E-MEETINGS OR NET CONFERENCING OPTIONS

Online services are now available, called *e-meetings*, in which you can meet with others without ever leaving your computer. Each person must have a camera or webcam attached to her computer. After all the participants log on, you can see everyone from your computer screen. This is a huge time-saver, especially if you have meeting participants who live on opposite sides of the country or overseas. All e-meeting services require you to have your own webcam and a high-speed Internet connection. You can purchase webcams from any local computer equipment store or online retailer. Then, you need to sign up for one of the e-meeting services listed here to connect everyone:

- **AIM@Work (www.aim.com)**—This American Online service allows online and teleconference meetings. With this service, only one person needs to be an AOL member; the other participants can be signed on as guests. An introductory offer of 500 free minutes is available.

- **Meetrix (www.meetrix.com)**—Meetrix is a service that enables real-time online meetings. This e-meeting service supports PowerPoint presentations and other application sharing, regardless of whether other participants have the software installed on their systems. A prepay option and a pay-as-you-go option are available.

- **MegaMeeting (www.megameeting.com)**—MegaMeeting is a web-based conference service that uses your current Internet browser and requires no additional software. This company charges a monthly rate that varies depending on the number of people you have during an e-meeting.

To do list

- ❑ Determine the who, what, when, and where details of the meeting.
- ❑ Place high-priority discussion topics at the beginning of the agenda.
- ❑ Establish time limits for all discussion topics.
- ❑ Designate a coordinator of the meeting for questions and managing confirmations.

Developing Agendas and Planning the Meeting

Planning a meeting does take time, but it's time well-spent. The planning you do can help ensure a successful meeting that increases participation and follow-through. When you know the purpose of the meeting, that purpose sets the stage for determining the when, what, who, and where of your meeting.

The purpose of the agenda is to clearly outline the plan for the meeting. Agenda content should include the details of the meeting's time, place, and attendees; the meeting's objective; and all the discussion topics to be covered. You can create either a formal or an informal agenda, depending on the type of meeting and number of participants

note Don't ever bypass developing an agenda for any meeting. Agendas provide the meeting framework for the leader and participants. When my clients complain of bad meetings, the first question I ask is "Did you have an agenda?" More often than not, the answer is "No." It is surprising that such a simple and necessary step for meeting management is usually bypassed.

you'll have. Formal agendas usually include much more content and information. Informal agendas typically just have quick bullet-point listings of discussion topics.

> **tip** Clear, concise, and detailed agendas help individuals prepare for the meeting and encourage everyone to stay on-track. If you find there is nothing to put on an agenda, maybe you don't need to meet.

Things You'll Need

☐   Computer

☐   Your master task list

☐   Access to your meeting note tablets

Setting the Agenda

There are some preliminary details to consider when creating the agenda, including when and where the meeting should be scheduled, what the meeting should accomplish, and who will attend. Giving thought to these issues is the first step toward planning a successful meeting.

What Should Be Accomplished at the Meeting?

Working from the meeting's stated purpose and objective, list the essential items that need to be discussed and accomplished. If you need to request agenda items from others, allow yourself at least two weeks before the meeting. This gives you enough time to prepare the agenda and plan accordingly.

To determine how long the meeting should last, consider the agenda items you've compiled and determine how long it might take to cover them. Make sure the discussion topics listed can fit into a realistic time frame. If not, you must consider planning additional meetings.

When Should the Meeting Be Scheduled?

If you're planning a recurring meeting, assess how often you need to meet—daily, weekly, or possibly monthly. Choose a time and day that fit the purpose of the meeting and the schedules of attendees. Tuesdays, Wednesdays, and Thursdays are usually good days to meet. Mondays and Fridays are days when many individuals take off for a long weekend or are busy trying to start or finish certain projects, so these days typically aren't good days for meetings. Mid-day (from 9 a.m. to 12 p.m.) and mid-afternoon (from 1 p.m. to 4 p.m.) are good times to meet for groups. One-on-one meetings seem to work well early in the morning or later in the afternoon. If you need participants to brainstorm or participate in thought-provoking discussions, you might benefit from scheduling the meeting in the morning when people will be fresh and alert. If the meeting is for conveying information, you can schedule it later in the afternoon. Try to avoid scheduling meetings right at the beginning or end of business hours when individuals are responding to and receiving communications via phone or email or trying to wrap things up for the day.

In most cases, however, you are subject to scheduling a meeting when the participants are available. Do your best to schedule it during the best time, or day, for everyone.

Who Will Attend?

Be clear about who needs to attend the meeting. Decide which attendees must be there to fully discuss the agenda topics or to move forward with decisions or tasks. If you feel you must invite some individuals strictly to avoid offending them, make it clear that their attendance is purely voluntary; then, they can decide whether to attend. If any of the essential participants cannot attend, reschedule the meeting to a time when every essential participant can attend.

Where Should I Hold a Meeting?

Most regular face-to-face meetings are held in office conference rooms. Depending on the type of meeting you are holding, you might want to hold it offsite from the company location. If you have participants coming from varying locations, try to pick the most convenient and centralized location for everyone. For all-day and strategic meetings, holding the meeting offsite can keep participants focused. Also, meetings that require brainstorming and creativity usually have better results outside the office location. As mentioned previously, be sure to consider the other alternatives to face-to-face meetings, such as phone conferences and e-meetings.

tip
For informal and quick meetings, consider having participants stand up during meetings in centralized locations. Standing meetings are often short and concise.

Writing the Agenda

At the top of all agendas, include the name of the meeting, date, location, and time. If not stated in the email notification, also list the confirmed participants. This basic detailed information located at the top of the agenda makes it easy for participants to plan to attend. If the agenda you send is merely a draft, be sure to note that clearly at the top; when you send a revision or final agenda, note the revised date so participants don't confuse it with previous versions.

Schedule the informational items first. Keep them brief and no longer than 5–10 minutes. This should include updates from the last meeting on action items and quick announcements. Primary discussion topics should be addressed next. Take advantage of the precious time you have with the group and address the highest-priority topics first, even if they take longer. Some people schedule lower-priority and quicker discussion items first to get them out of the way quickly. But this plan can backfire and leave you with too little time to discuss the most important topics. Often, lower-priority items not covered in a meeting are more easily postponed or can be resolved by one or two individuals. Leave the last 5–10 minutes at the end of the meeting for a wrap-up of action items, next steps, and plans for the next meeting.

Be sure you assign who will guide each discussion topic so those individuals are prepared to lead that part of the discussion. Make sure you ask those particular individuals whether they have any special requests, such as AV needs, easels, handouts, or other visuals or equipment. Figure 9.1 shows a sample agenda.

FIGURE 9.1
Shown here is a sample meeting agenda created in the Microsoft Word Agenda Wizard. At www.office.microsoft.com, Microsoft offers agenda templates and wizards to help you create agendas. Click Templates directly underneath the left sidebar on the home page. Once on the Template page, in the top search toolbar, type the word *agenda*. This gives you a list of multiple types of agenda templates and wizards available to download free.

Monthly Staff Meeting	December 6, 2005 1:00-3:00pm Conference Room A
Revised 11/28/05	

Confirmed Attendees: Alycia, Sally, Keith, Tom, Regina, Jackie
Please read before the meeting: Attached documents
Please bring to the meeting: Agenda items for strategic meeting

Agenda

1.	Reminder of Holiday Party	Sally	1:00-1:02
2.	Update of action items from November staff meeting	Alycia	1:02-1:15
3.	Update of re-organization of company	Alycia	1:15-1:45
4.	Review of agenda for 2006 Annual Strategic Meeting	Alycia	1:45-2:15
5.	Review of year-to-date financials of department	Keith	2:15-2:35
6.	Review of process of submitting year-end invoices/bills	Keith	2:35-2:45
7.	Reminder to use new forms (questions and clarifications)	Sally	2:45-2:50
8.	Review of this month's action items	Alycia	2:50-2:55
9.	Reminder of time & date of next month's meeting	Sally	2:55-2:57
10.	Wrap-up, closing remarks and thank-you to attendees	Alycia	2:57-3:00

Additional Information

Setting Clear Time Limits and Scheduling Breaks

Be sure you include a start and end time on the agenda, and propose estimated discussion times for each topic. Setting this framework assures participants that the meeting won't drag on forever and encourages everyone to stick to the proposed limits for each discussion item. Knowing there is a time limit encourages everyone to stay on-track to complete the agenda.

Give updates a smaller amount of time during the meeting. Most people will have received updates through emails and other correspondence, so meeting updates should only be brief recaps. If you have too many lengthy discussion items to cover in the meeting, either extend the meeting or move some items to a subsequent meeting.

tip If you plan meetings regularly, track future agenda items for the next meeting as you think of them. Write them in the notes field in your electronic calendar entry, or write them next to the appointment in your paper planner. Before you write the agenda, refer to your notes in your calendar. This will save time trying to remember what you wanted to put on the agenda.

After about 1–2 hours of meeting time, most individuals need a 10- or 15-minute break. This gives all participants a mental and physical break from the meeting and an opportunity to listen to voice mail and review email. If you're scheduling an all-day meeting, be sure to include a few longer breaks and a meal break.

After time limits are established, if you need to extend the meeting, make sure you have agreement from the group. Ask the following question, "We have these further agenda items to discuss, which will probably take 30 more minutes. We can either extend our meeting another 30 minutes or defer these agenda items to our next meeting. Which option would work best for everyone?" This allows participants the courtesy to end or extend the meeting by consensus.

TIPS FOR THOSE WHO ARE LATE TO MEETINGS

We have all been culprits at one time or another—being late to a meeting. Sometimes it can't be helped. Most times, however, people are late because they lose track of time or are unable to stop what they're doing at the moment. Here are some suggestions to encourage people to be on time for your meetings:

- **Always, always start on time**—If you always start on time, people will expect it.

- **Consider starting your meetings not on the hour or half hour**—Research suggests that meetings that start at odd times, such as 3:45, are more likely to have people arrive on time.

- **Get a bell and ring it**—Depending on your office configuration, get a bell or other noisemaker and ring it 2 minutes before the meeting begins. The bell sound usually reminds individuals of the old school days when that bell rang and they had to run to get to class on time. Pavlov's dog trick just might work!

- **Send an email just before the meeting and insert the important or priority icon**—Often people are in the midst of responding to email and wanting to finish that one last email before the meeting starts. Reminding others via email is a good way to get them to wrap-up their current email response and come to the meeting.

- **Those who are consistently late go on the agenda first**—If you have a few individuals who are always late, consider putting them on the agenda first. This creates accountability and responsibility to get to the meeting on time.

Notifying Participants

Ideally, it is best to give written notification of the meeting as soon as it is planned to give all participants ample time to schedule it in their calendars. Send participants a copy of the agenda and any supplementary documents at least one week prior to the meeting. This gives participants time to think about the meeting and come prepared. State in the notification that participants should send any additional information to all other attendees before the meeting or bring copies to the meeting.

Designate a coordinator of the meeting who manages the email questions and confirmations from participants. This could be you, the meeting planner, or an administrative assistant. Ask that participants confirm attendance with the designated coordinator only. This eliminates the multiple reply all email responses that become unnecessary email for others to manage. Establishing one coordinator also eliminates the email confusion of who will address the questions or concerns about a meeting, also eliminating unnecessary email trains.

Most email programs, such as Outlook, ACT!, and Lotus Notes, provide an electronic tool for sending meeting announcements to all participants. The individual sending the meeting announcement creates a new calendar entry and then invites attendees by inserting their email addresses in the To field provided (see Figure 9.2).

Each invited participant receives an email notification of the meeting, as shown in Figure 9.3. Sending a meeting invitation through this function allows individuals to accept or decline the invitation to the meeting. When the receiver accepts or declines the meeting, an automatic email response is generated to the sender, allowing easy tracking of confirmations from participants.

If the participant uses the same email software, accepting the invitation automatically adds the meeting to the participant's electronic calendar, along with all the email text information (including attachments), in the notes section of the calendar entry. This feature eliminates the need for attendees to manually enter the meeting into their calendars.

FIGURE 9.2

Shown here is an example of a meeting announcement created in the new calendar window in Outlook. To send a meeting invitation to other participants in Outlook, click the Invite Attendees icon in the toolbar located in the new calendar entry window. A To line is inserted to add other participants' email addresses.

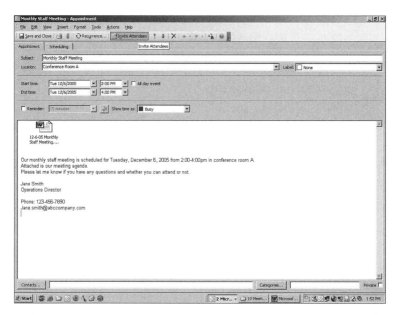

FIGURE 9.3

Shown here is a meeting invitation sent and received through Outlook. Click the Accept button located at the top of the email, and Outlook automatically adds the meeting to your Outlook calendar. A separate window also opens and asks whether you would like to send an automatic reply to the sender. Select Send a Response Now and click OK. An automatic email response is then generated to the sender, with **Accepted** or **Declined** in the subject line for easy tracking.

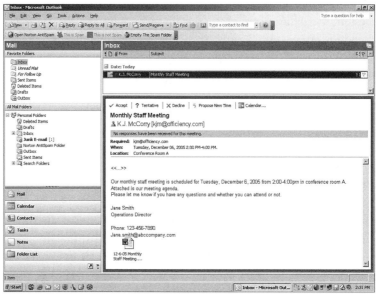

If you do a lot of meeting planning, you can use software that provides further help with planning meeting logistics and registration:

- **Certain Software (www.certain.com)**—This software developer offers Meeting Planning Plus, which manages all the details of a meeting. Certain Software also has special software called Register123 that manages registrations.

- **Ekeba International (www.ekeba.com)**—Its software, Complete Event Manager, also helps you manage the full logistics of meetings and is a less-expensive option to other sophisticated meeting planning software.

- **Event Management** Systems (www.dea.com)—One of its software products, EMS Lite, helps you with room scheduling. This is particularly useful in an office setting where multiple conference rooms need to be scheduled.

- **Net Simplicity (www.netsimplicity.com)**—Its software, Meeting Room Manager, is good for scheduling meeting and conference rooms.

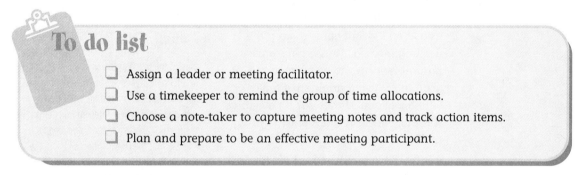

To do list

- ☐ Assign a leader or meeting facilitator.
- ☐ Use a timekeeper to remind the group of time allocations.
- ☐ Choose a note-taker to capture meeting notes and track action items.
- ☐ Plan and prepare to be an effective meeting participant.

Assigning Meeting Roles and Functions

Meetings that have no structure or assigned roles can become little more than frustrating time traps. It is important that you choose a leader, note-taker, and time-keeper at each meeting to ensure that the meeting is productive, stays on-track, and produces real and lasting results. Sometimes, all those roles can be filled by one person; other times, though, multiple people will fill the roles. Everyone who attends a meeting serves at least one role—that of participant. When every participant performs his role successfully, a meeting can be a productive use of time.

Things You'll Need

- ☐ A copy of Robert's Rules of Order
- ☐ Note-taking tools, such as a writing pad and pen, a laptop computer, or a voice recorder

Filling the Leader or Facilitator Role

The leader or facilitator is the person who guides the discussion of the meeting. This role is key to the success of all meetings. The leader/facilitator should not dominate a meeting, but rather serve as the conductor who ensures the meeting and its participants stay on-track. The leader needs to be the catalyst to ensure that everyone at the meeting is involved and participating. This person can be the manager or supervisor of the group, or even someone outside the group, if that is more appropriate for the meeting content. The leader/facilitator should perform the following functions during a meeting:

- **State the objective of the meeting and review the agenda**—The first thing a leader/facilitator should do is make sure everyone has an agenda and any other meeting handouts. The leader begins the meeting with a review of the purpose and goals of the meeting, the discussion points to be covered, and a reminder to participants of the scheduled closing time of the meeting.

- **Keep the meeting on-track**—The leader/facilitator should use the agenda as a checklist and guide to keep the meeting focused. Most groups have a natural tendency to go off on a tangent, introducing unplanned topics or telling personal stories during meetings. It is the leader's responsibility to bring the discussion back on-track. To do so, restate the goal, purpose, and objective of the meeting. Also, provide a brief recap of what has been discussed, decided, and still pending. This guides the conversation back to the agenda. If the sidetrack discussion is about an important topic not on the agenda, the leader should ask the participants to decide whether to either continue the discussion or table the discussion for another meeting (or the leader can make the decision herself).

> **tip**
> If you are the facilitator, let the participants know at the beginning of the meeting that you will interrupt or intervene if you feel the conversation has gone off track. When this becomes necessary, be gentle in your interruption, thank the person for his comments and feedback, and ask that the conversation return to the topic at hand. Make others accountable for the meeting's success by encouraging them to remind you if the meeting has gone off track or over the allotted time for a particular topic.

- **Encourage others to be involved with the meeting**—Be open to the suggestions and opinions of all group members. Ask those who have not participated whether they have any comments or thoughts. If a few individuals have a tendency to dominate the meeting, ask them to allow others to speak. Sometimes allowing just a few seconds of silence encourages others to make comments.

- **Assign and delegate tasks/action items and due dates**—Be sure to assign each action step mentioned in the meeting to a specific individual(s) and agree on deadline dates. Unless you assign each task to a specific person, the item can go unfinished and the meeting's participants can become frustrated with a lack of progress. Be certain to confirm the method in which those responsible for action items are to notify the leader (or someone else) when the action is completed; this notification might be via email, a phone call, or an update at the next meeting.

- **Summarize the discussion**—Review (or ask that the note-taker to review) in brief what was discussed and decided at the end of the meeting. Review all decisions and conclusions to each discussion topic on the agenda. Clearly itemize the tasks that need to be done and state who is going to do each. This summary encourages all the participants to leave the meeting with a sense of purpose and accomplishment.

> **tip** At the conclusion of the meeting, be sure to say "thank you" to all the participants for their time, involvement, opinions, and insights. Everyone wants to be appreciated and thanked for their time.

- **Assess the meeting**—If you are leading or facilitating new meetings, you might want to ask participants of this meeting for feedback, either verbally or through a written evaluation of how the meeting went. If the group or organization has a history of unsuccessful meetings, getting feedback can help ensure the success of future meetings, while giving you input on your role as a leader and facilitator.

Robert's Rules of Order (www.robertsrules.com) is a guidebook written about formal parliamentary procedures for effectively guiding meetings. Establishing Robert's Rules in your meeting can be highly effective, especially if you have no knowledge or experience running meetings or have difficult meetings to run. The guidebook has answers and procedures for just about every situation you might encounter in a meeting. Robert's Rules are typically used during formal meetings, such as board of directors meetings.

CREATING GROUND RULES AT MEETINGS

Setting up guidelines, or ground rules, governing the protocol of meeting participation can help you run a more efficient meeting. Developing meeting ground rules to be followed by all the participants is an especially good idea for new groups or meetings in which sensitive topics will be discussed. When a group establishes and agrees to guidelines, everyone becomes accountable for enforcing the rules.

Here are some examples of possible meeting guidelines to adopt:

- No cell phone or PDA use during a meeting. (An exception might be to allow ringers to be turned to vibrate for urgencies and emergencies.)
- No sidebar conversations with others.
- The meeting will start and end on time, with breaks.
- Let one person talk at a time. Minimize interruptions of others.
- Defer unrelated issues and topics to be resolved at a later date. Some groups like to coin those items be put in a "parking lot."
- Keep the discussion focused and on track.
- Make decisions by consensus (or majority).
- Make statements, and then invite questions and comments.
- Be open to everyone's opinion and suggestions.

Assigning a Timekeeper

The timekeeper is responsible for making sure each discussion topic stays within the allotted time. This individual reminds those who are speaking how much time they have remaining on each topic and gives the leader periodic updates on the time remaining in the overall meeting. The timekeeper reminds everyone to stay on-track and limits interruptions and disturbances during meetings.

The leader/facilitator can also assume the timekeeper role, or it can be assigned to another meeting participant. I suggest rotating the role of timekeeper among participants throughout subsequent meetings. This rotation encourages all participants to be aware of the time and to share accountability for keeping the meeting on schedule.

tip Take your calendar with you to meetings, so you have your schedule with you when it comes time to set up the next meeting. Rather than emailing or phoning to set up the next meeting, it's more efficient to do it at the close of the current meeting. Scheduling subsequent meetings is much easier when all participants have their calendars in front of them.

Using a Note-Taker

Most group meetings should have meeting notes taken and distributed. Generating formal written meeting notes serves two primary purposes: First, it provides an accurate record of what transpired for historical purposes and for those individuals who could not attend. Second, it can be used to verify action items assigned and decisions made during the meeting so there is no confusion on those points at future meetings.

Trying to determine what happened at a previous meeting can be extremely frustrating when there is no formal written record. Having meeting notes resolves discrepancies over these points that might arise at future meetings.

I recommend typing meeting notes into a laptop during the meeting or recording the meeting on tape, if possible. This saves the hassle of transcribing handwritten notes later. Sometimes, individuals can't read their writing or forget the complete train of thought on a discussion topic, especially if the note-taker waited too long to type the notes. Save time, and type meeting notes at the meeting. This then provides immediate access to the notes for other participants and those who could not attend the meeting.

The note-taker can be an assigned role, such as that of a formal secretary at board of director meetings, or it can be rotated among participants. Some meetings have one person whose sole purpose is tracking the meeting notes; that person doesn't participate in the meeting discussion so he can concentrate solely on recording what is being discussed and decided. In addition to resolving discrepancies and generating a record of the meeting's events, the note-taker also can help the group clarify discussions that become confusing, help participants reach consensus on next action steps, and distribute and file the meeting notes.

Recording Discussions and Clarifying Decisions

Every discussion item needs to have some sort of resolution, decision, or conclusion. Often, however, a discussion ventures off-track or jumps to the next agenda item without clear resolution, leaving meeting participants with no conclusion or understanding of decisions made about the discussion topic. The meeting notes must include the key points of the discussion and the reasoning behind any conclusion or decision that was reached. If the discussion becomes confusing and it is unclear what has been decided or why, the note-taker should speak up to ask for that clarity. The note-taker should state what he understands from the conversation and ask the group whether that understanding is accurate.

Use the original agenda to capture meeting notes, so the format is standard and easy to refer to later. The note-taker should capture notes on each agenda item and discussion topic. Even if there was no discussion on a particular agenda item, the lack of discussion should be recorded in the meeting notes. The notes should include information on each discussion topic and the key points of the discussion, including the pros and cons commented on. If a particular topic remains unresolved at the end of the meeting, the note-taker must ask for and record the next steps the group would like to take to reach a conclusion on that issue. The note-taker should ensure that, for each discussion point on the agenda, highlighted points of the discussion are clear and accurate in written form. In addition, the final decision, the conclusion, and any future follow-up actions should be noted in the meeting notes.

Summarizing and Recording Next Action Steps

The note-taker should create one master task list from all the action items determined at the meeting. With each action item, the note-taker records the person responsible for accomplishing the item and the due date. This summarized action list could be distributed in the following manner for easy access and visibility for others to remember:

- Include in the body of the email the summarized task list with the meeting notes attached.

- Put the summarized task list at the top of the meeting notes so it is on the first page, versus the last page, which is harder to see.

- Integrate the tasks into another common shared task list the team uses. It might be located in a separate document; project software; or a shared task list within a PIM, such as Outlook or Lotus Notes.

After the meeting notes have been distributed and action items clarified, the group needs to agree to a mechanism of follow-up and accountability for those action items. If the meeting is a regularly scheduled meeting, follow-up can occur at the next scheduled time. If this meeting was a one-time-only meeting, determine a follow-up plan with your colleagues on how the action steps will be handled. This ensures that those actions will be handled and not delayed or forgotten. Nothing is more frustrating than attending a meeting, determining next action steps, and then everything being forgotten when the meeting concludes. Take the next step and determine a follow-up plan before the meeting concludes.

Distributing and Filing Notes

Ideally, meeting notes should be distributed no later than one week after the meeting. Others who were not present at the meeting can use the notes to catch up on the status of topics discussed at the meeting. Having meeting notes soon after also serves as a reminder of the committed action items each person is accountable for.

Save the meeting notes electronically in a common shared drive so everyone has access to them. Because meeting notes are date-related, I suggest developing a standard naming convention in which the date is always entered first, preceded by the type of meeting and any other data you need in the filename. An example is **12-06-2005 Staff Meeting Notes**. This way, you can easily see meeting notes in chronological order for reference. (Refer to Figure 9.2 for an example.)

Being an Effective Participant

Even if you are not the facilitator, note-taker, or timekeeper, you have a job. Your job is to participate in the meeting. Being an active participant is important for ensuring the success of meetings. Everyone should know the basic skills used to conduct effective meetings to assist in keeping meetings on-track, focused, and productive.

Participants need to participate fully and be respectful in the meeting. They should bring to the meeting an open mind and listen to what is being discussed. They should respect others' differences of opinion and ideas. If you disagree, ask questions of your colleagues first to better understand their position. If you are an extrovert, be sure not to dominate the meeting. If you are more introverted, be sure you let others hear your opinions. Be mindful not to interrupt others while speaking, and refrain from sidebar conversations with the person next to you while someone else is speaking. The golden rule of "treat others as you want to be treated" is something to remember when participating in meetings. And be on time. Let's say it again, be on time!

tip Responding to email or phone calls during a meeting is considered impolite, unless permission has been granted by all group members or the leader/facilitator of the meeting. Refrain from looking at your handheld or phone during the meeting. It gives others the signal that you don't care and do not want to be involved. Make sure you request breaks to allow time to respond to email and phone communications. If you have urgent matters that require you to respond during a meeting, let others know this at the beginning of the meeting.

Make sure you have read the agenda and come prepared with information, as needed or requested. If the agenda requires some brainstorming or ideas, be sure you have given those issues thought and come prepared to present your ideas. If attachments and handouts have been sent, take the time to review them before the meeting to help maximize discussion.

DEALING WITH PROBLEMS DURING MEETINGS

A wide variety of personalities in a group can present problems during a meeting. Most individuals are not aware of their behavior or need gentle reminders. Here are a few suggestions to help with common problems during meetings:

- **Talkers**—Talkers are individuals who seem to go on and on and have difficulty getting to the point. Ask them before they start talking to summarize their comments in 3–4 minutes, or any other appropriate limited time.

- **Dominators**—Dominators are individuals who always seem to have the "right" answer and dominate the discussion. Before they start talking, tell them that you appreciate their input but would like to hear from some other people in the room. Ask the dominator directly who else in the meeting would offer some good insight to the discussion at hand. It forces him to make the decision of who will talk next.

- **Wanderers**—Wanderers are individuals who go off the agenda and begin to discuss unrelated topics, issues, and problems. Ask the wanderer whether she thinks the topic she has introduced is relevant for the meeting. Give her other options for addressing that particular issue, such as asking that the issue or topic be deferred to the agenda of the next meeting or be handled by a designated individual at a later date.

- **Outbursters**—Outbursters are individuals who seem to explode or get angry at meetings. Tell the exploder you understand he is angry and frustrated, and repeat his position to him so he feels he has been heard. This sometimes diffuses the anger by acknowledging it and causing the outburster to think about his behavior. Ask the group whether it agrees with the person's thoughts. If so, get others' opinion. If not, ask that the discussion move back to the agenda. If the behavior is completely disruptive, it might be best to ask the person to leave the meeting for a short time or altogether.

To do list

- ❑ Write your meeting notes in your computer or spiral notebook as opposed to a legal pad.
- ❑ Track your action items from a meeting in your task list.
- ❑ Build accountability with your team

Tracking Individual Meeting Notes

Even if you are not the designated note-taker, most individuals like to keep their own meeting notes. Individual meeting notes usually include discussion points, personal action items, and other miscellaneous data an individual wants to remember. Meeting notes can often get lost or forgotten. Remember that information is only as good as is its accessibility. Develop a method of tracking your individual meeting notes so the data does not become lost or forgotten.

Things You'll Need

- ❑ Day planner or calendar
- ❑ Note-taking tools, such as spiral-bound notebooks, a pen/pencil, and a laptop or notebook computer
- ❑ Word processing software

Tracking Personal Action Items

Note and record your action item in your designated task list at the moment it has been assigned. Action items are the number-one piece of information that gets lost in meeting notes. You might plan to add tasks to your task list after the meeting, but this just creates one more thing for you to do. When you get back to your desk after a meeting, you have email, phone messages, and colleagues all waiting for your time. Often, your good intentions to put those action items in your task list get delayed; then the tasks are forgotten. Simplify things by bringing your task list to the meeting and recording your action items during the meeting, as they are assigned. This habit will save you time and the hassle of trying to track action items after the meeting.

Coding Your Meeting Notes

Be sure to date and code your meeting notes. Write the date and name of the meeting in upper-right corner of the paper pad for easy retrieval in the future. If you decide you want to track your action items in your meeting notes and not in your task list, consider coding those action items for easy reference. You can draw a star icon next to the action item or write the letter *A* next to it to stand for *action*. Another idea is to bring a highlighter to the meeting and highlight those action items in your meeting notes. If you have other pieces of information you write during a meeting, consider other consistent coding methods so information stands out.

Capturing Meeting Notes on Paper

Most individuals still like to handwrite meeting notes for a couple of reasons. First is the ease and quickness with which most of us can write. Second, writing notes has just become habit. If you are going to handwrite meeting notes, consider using a spiral notebook instead of a legal pad. A spiral notebook allows you to easily turn to the next page and keep meeting notes in a chronological manner. After half of a legal pad has been used, the remaining pages have a tendency to flip down easily, making it difficult to record on the last half of the tablet. Also, consider having one notebook for each type of reoccurring meeting. This makes it easier to refer to previous notes in the same notebook. If you maintain multiple notebooks for a number of meetings, be sure you keep all of them in an easy-to-reach place on your desk, so you can quickly grab the correct one as you are running to the meeting.

Capturing Meeting Notes Electronically

With laptops being so prevalent these days, consider taking your laptop to meetings and recording your notes electronically. This is especially helpful for individuals who type well. Taking notes electronically allows you to keep one document per meeting, eliminating the need to manage paper tablets. Also, if you use an electronic task list, typing on your laptop is easier than typing on the handheld. The other advantage to having your laptop at a meeting is the ability to reference other documents electronically. This saves the hassle of carrying paper files and notebooks to each meeting.

Computer manufacturers now make tablet PCs that have the capability to record handwritten characters and convert them into typed text in a Word document. This is especially useful for those who still like to handwrite and also want their meeting notes in an electronic format. For more information, product reviews, and comparisons on tablet PCs, visit the following websites: Tablet PC2 (www.tabletpc2.com) and Tablet PC Talk (www.tabletpctalk.com).

When saving your electronic meeting notes, consider setting up a folder(s) within your directory and using a standard naming convention for documents. If you want to see your notes in chronological order, first insert the date in numerical format and then enter the name of the meeting—for example, **01-05-2006 Project Meeting Notes-Marketing Department**. If you have regular meetings, consider creating a subfolder named with the year, and save all your meeting notes per each year, as shown in Figure 9.4. This arrangement lets you more easily view notes historically rather than in one line for multiple years.

tip

If you have repetitive text, phrases, or words you want to appear with the touch of a few strokes, use the AutoText function in Microsoft Word. Open Word and type a word or phrase you would like to be automatically inserted. Highlight the word or phrase and select Insert, Auto Text, New. A new window opens with the text you highlighted inserted. Add or edit your text in the line provided and then click OK. When you begin typing the first few letters of that word or phrase, Word automatically inserts the full text for you. This is a great time-saver if you have a lot of repetitive phrases or words you need to type in a document.

FIGURE 9.4

Here is an example of how to save meeting notes electronically. Consider creating a subfolder for each year. Then, create a standard naming convention with the date inserted first numerically, so the meeting notes stay in chronological order.

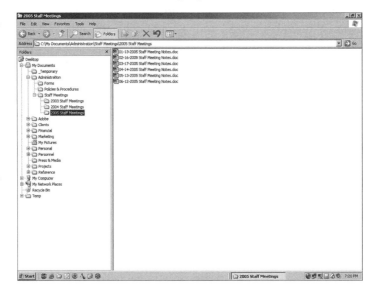

Summary

Meetings are part of everyday business life and can be the source of some great ideas, thoughts, and momentum. But effective meetings take planning. Before you call a meeting, be sure you have something to meet about. Be prepared and create an agenda before the meeting. Assign the roles of leader, timekeeper, and note-taker to a specific individual or individuals. Once there, remind everyone of their roles, the time commitment, and the purpose for which they are there. Finally, thank everyone for their involvement and follow through on the actions everyone committed to taking. The more attentive you are to planning and conducting meetings, the more payoff you'll see from the time you spend in them. Here are a few reminders before planning your next meeting:

- Don't plan a meeting without being clear about why you need to meet.
- Always have an agenda for every meeting.
- Consider assigning roles in each meeting, and encourage everyone to participate.
- Create standard meeting guidelines to ensure effective participation.
- Don't let your action items get lost in your meeting notes; add them to your own task list.
- Bring your laptop to meetings and take meeting notes electronically.

In the next and final chapter, "Making the Most of Your Day," we discuss how to get it all done amidst meetings, phone calls, emails, and interruptions. It is difficult in today's business world to focus on your priorities with communications surrounding you every minute. We also talk about how to manage all the sabotages on your day and how to accomplish the things that matter most to you.

Making the Most of
Your Day

In this chapter:

* Learn how to plan your day and get done what matters most

* Discover ways to reduce interruptions and manage your schedule

* Determine the best way to track and manage your incoming and outgoing phone calls

Remember back to a time when you didn't have a cell phone or a computer on your desk and a handheld was just something you could carry? And what was Microsoft? This period of time wasn't so long ago; even 10 years ago we were not inundated with the workplace technology that we have today. This new technology has improved the workplace in so many ways, but most of us have had to relearn ways in which to manage the flood of communications, information, and tasks that go along with it.

The American workforce is hard at work every day. We are working harder, longer, and faster than ever before in our country's history. So, why don't we feel that we're getting things accomplished? Most individuals feel that their days are consumed with all the unavoidable external factors we must deal with each day, such as meetings, email, mail, phone calls, interruptions, and crises. Thus, most people aren't able to get done what they want to get done. Not having control over your work day can leave you feeling exhausted, overwhelmed, and stressed.

Developing organization and internal office systems provides more control over those external factors and helps you focus on what you want to get done. Being organized does not mean that all those daily items, such as meetings and communications, will go away—they won't! But you *can* manage and control them so they don't overtake your work day. In this chapter, we discuss how you can best manage and make the most of your day. You'll have read some of these ideas in earlier chapters, but we've collected them here to emphasize their importance for organizing and maximizing the precious hours of your working day.

To do list

- ❏ Plan your day and determine the 10 actions you want to complete.
- ❏ Review your task list daily and determine whether to delete, defer, or do each item.
- ❏ Complete an action item before beginning the next one.
- ❏ Understand your own procrastination habits.

The Best Way to Manage Your Action Items

Chapter 5, "Using Your Contact Software to Its Full Potential," discussed optional ways to track and organize action items. In that chapter, you learned how to choose and use an area to consolidate and track your action items in a task list; you might track action items, for example, in an electronic task list, a day planner, or another type of document. Having one task list to review, as opposed to having jottings on scattered bits of paper and Post-it notes, makes it easier to review and plan your day. The hard part is actually getting all the tasks on your to-do list done! That is why reviewing your action list and planning your day is so essential.

In today's multitasking world, mastering the art of completion is an essential step to achieving accomplishment. Completing action items is very rewarding because it gives you a sense of closure and accomplishment and energizes you to move onto the next task. Without completion, your work day can leave you feeling tired, stressed, and discouraged. No matter how many tasks you have going at the same time, get in the habit of completing the things you begin.

Things You'll Need

- ❏ Task list
- ❏ Contact management or personal information management software, day planner
- ❏ Computer
- ❏ Pen and paper

Planning Your Day and Week

To get the items on your action list accomplished, you must take time to plan your day and week. Look at the bigger picture of everything you need to do and what you need to focus on now, this day, or this week. This involves looking at not only your task list, but also your email inbox, phone log, calendar, and paper on your desk.

Assigning due dates or priority, as we also discussed in Chapter 5, gives you the information you need to plan your day. You don't have to try to accomplish your entire to-do list; you only need to address those items that you have scheduled to do this day or week.

Planning should not take more than 5–10 minutes daily. This small investment in planning time helps save you time throughout your work day. Planning also enables you to be clearer in your approach to your work and helps you to focus on what is important.

Planning enables you to structure your day around achieving what you most want to accomplish within it. By remaining focused on your priorities, you are less prone to allowing urgencies to run your day. Review your action areas of email, paper, calendar, phone log, and task list and determine not more than 10 top items you must get done that day (or week). You can create a separate list of those 10 actions, highlight them on your to-do list, or code them electronically; use whatever method helps you focus on those 10 items. In reviewing your action areas and creating your list of top 10 to-dos, make these determinations for each action item:

- **Delete**—Delete those tasks that, for whatever reason, have become obsolete or no longer necessary.

- **Defer**—If an action item needn't be completed today or this week, defer the item to a future due date. Be sure to set a new due date, however; doing so forces you to review that task again at a later time so it doesn't get lost or forgotten. Be careful of repeatedly deferring an action item. At one point, you either need to do it or need to delete it.

- **Do**—Add this to your top 10 list and take action on the task today or this week.

> **note** I suggest not picking more than 10 items per day, but that number might not be right for your action items or working style. Use your judgment to decide the number of action items appropriate for you and your work day.

Completing Your Action Items

After you determine your plan for the day or week, do your best to keep focused on the tasks at hand. It is ideal if you can complete one task before moving on to the next task. Multitasking, although common in today's workplace, can be difficult and frustrating for some people to manage. If you begin to get in the habit of starting with the first task and completing it before you begin the next one, you will find that you stay more focused on the action items that you have planned to do.

But that's the ideal, and few of us operate in an ideal work environment. When you need to multitask, don't allow yourself to become scattered and disorganized. Find a stopping point with your current task and jot a note of where to begin when you return. Then, handle the more immediate task. Make a list of the things you need to do and then assign them a numbered priority; renumber as necessary if priorities shift and remember to mark completed tasks off the list.

If you have a hard time completing tasks, make sure the task itself is a reasonable and doable task. If the task is extensive and complex or will take more time than you have to give that day or week, break the task into its logical steps and list them in order. Place action verbs in front of your action items to create a list of specific steps you must perform. For example, if you write on your to-do list only "Plan annual meeting", that doesn't make clear what you specifically need to do. What is the first action step you need to take to plan the annual meeting? Maybe it is "Write the agenda" or "Schedule a conference room"; both of those action items are more doable steps that you can complete in a reasonable amount of time.

If you feel you can't complete a task in the time you have, set a time limit for working on that item; do what you can during that time, and schedule a time to return and complete the task. If you need to work on the annual budget, for example, and you think completing it might take you an hour but you don't have that much time to spare, you still can make headway with this task. Make a decision to stick with it for 30 minutes and then move on to other essential tasks. Doing a task in smaller chunks gets you closer to completion, avoids procrastination, and helps you maintain control of your time and schedule.

Although you needn't stop your current task to handle every new action item that comes your way, you do need to immediately schedule a due date for all incoming items. If you just look at new items and then move them off to the side while you continue to work on your current tasks, you might find that suddenly you have a huge stack of things to do, with no idea of where they fall within your priorities—with still more action items coming at you all the time. No matter if the action item enters your world as paper, as email, or through verbal requests, the sooner you assign a due date to the items, the faster they'll get in the queue and the better you'll be able to maintain your daily organization. Also, as we discussed in past chapters, be sure to store the details and documents of your action items in the proper locations until you are ready to take action.

tip Determine the best times in your week to have focused and uninterrupted time to work on your action items. I suggest creating at least one hour per day of uninterrupted time. You should block out the time in your calendar. This serves as a visual reminder that that space in the day is yours. If you share calendars, it also lets your colleagues know that you are unavailable.

Managing Procrastination

We all have lots of excuses for not getting things done. We feel overwhelmed or over-worked and just have too much to do. No matter how we justify it, however, procras-tination is still an unproductive habit. The key to conquering this bad habit is discovering why and when you procrastinate and then addressing those barriers. Following are some guidelines for overcoming and avoiding procrastination:

- **Remember that you don't need perfection; just do your best**—We all want to do our best, and some of us want to do every task perfectly. However, achieving that perfection might take more time and resources than are cur-rently available, so the task gets delayed. Instead of dragging out or avoiding the task in search of perfection, set reasonable goals, do your best, and get the job done efficiently and on time.

- **Be realistic with the resources you have available**—Sometimes we get stuck waiting for the ideal situation, resources, or time to complete an action. We tell ourselves that if we wait a few months, then—and only then—will the calendar be empty and we'll be able to concentrate solely on a particular project. Or, if we wait till next year, additional funds will be available for a particular project. Two months or next year come and the calendar is filled, a crisis has ensued, and there doesn't seem to be the extra cash flow we had hoped for. Instead of waiting for the ideal situation, brainstorm various ways a task could be performed. Then, consider the most realistic possibility and begin in that direction.

- **Break the task into smaller, bite-size chunks**—Some projects and tasks are so complex that they require more time than you have available in any one block. Consider breaking down the task or project into smaller tasks that take no more than 10–15 minutes each. These become doable steps that can be worked into your calendar and work day.

- **Just take a small step**—Sometimes we can become frozen as we try to envi-sion how to accomplish a difficult task. Sometimes just the act of beginning a task helps alleviate procrastination and begins to jog the mind forward. Create a Word document and use it to record brainstorming ideas, or simply list bullet points about the topic at hand. That small step can help you become clearer about what you need to do and how you can best accomplish the task. Thus, try to take a small action on even the most difficult task right away.

- **Make the best decision possible and move on**—No one is ever completely certain of an outcome, so we all have to make the best choices we can with the information and data we have. If you procrastinate about making deci-sions, think to yourself, "If you had to make a decision right now, what would that decision be?" Sometimes asking it in that framework encourages you to make a decision. If you have too many choices, limit them to the best two or three and make a decision from those reduced options. If all that fails, find a trusted colleague with whom can discuss decisions.

To do list

- ❏ Consolidate meetings in one time frame, when possible.
- ❏ Build in time gaps between meetings to deal with daily communications.
- ❏ Confirm all appointments and meetings one week prior.
- ❏ Develop your own plan for managing interruptions.

Things You'll Need

- ❏ Calendar
- ❏ Contact management or personal information management software, day planner
- ❏ Computer
- ❏ Pen and paper
- ❏ File folders, three-ring notebooks, plastic trays

Managing Your Schedule and Interruptions

Now that you know what you want to get done, you need to create the time in your week to get it done. Establish time during your week during which you can give your attention to the tasks at hand. Managing your schedule in this way helps you accomplish items.

Daily interruptions are also a large factor in not being able to get things done. In the 1970s the concept of the open-door policy was developed, which was supposed to encourage communication and approachability within the hierarchal structure of the workplace. This open-door policy has now turned into constant interruptions that limit our productivity. There are multiple ways to guard against interruptions, especially during those times we need to be focused.

Reviewing Your Calendar

Meetings and appointments can be time-consuming and disruptive. If possible, try to schedule and consolidate the majority of meetings and appointments on one, or two, days only. Then, the remaining week is available to get projects and other important action items accomplished. If that is impossible, split your day and either start or end with meetings, but try to avoid chopping up your schedule. It makes it more difficult to get the blocks of time you need to accomplish your tasks.

Build in time gaps of 15 minutes between meetings and appointments. This gives you time to organize the information you just received and enter new tasks and information into your handheld, planner, or meeting notebook. It also gives you time to deal with urgent communications. This gap also provides a buffer between appointments in case they run late (which often happens!). You then avoid being constantly late throughout the day with time gaps inserted.

Review your upcoming weekly calendar appointments on Monday or during the week before. Make confirmation calls or send confirmation emails to all your appointments verifying the date, time, and meeting place. That way, you avoid preparing for a meeting that has been cancelled, and you remind others that you are on their calendar.

After you have confirmed appointments, determine what you need to do to prepare, such as gathering materials for the meeting. If you bring your laptop to the meeting, make sure you have all necessary electronic documentation stored on it. If you prefer to work with paper documents, print them ahead of time and take them with you. Here are some of the documents you should bring to meetings:

- Agenda and handouts
- Directions to the meeting
- Additional material you want to share at the meeting
- Company information

Determine a location of where you want to store your meeting paperwork for the week. Here are some suggestions:

- Create separate a file folder for each meeting.
- Create one file folder for all the meetings you have in one week.
- Place documents in your meeting notebook or attaché case.
- Place documents in your day planner.
- Create five trays for each day of the week, and place documents in the corresponding day's tray.

CREATING NEW HABITS

Changing your work and organizational processes takes effort, but saves you much precious time in the long-run. Statistics estimate it takes 21 days to form a new habit, with it being repeated every day. Studies have also indicated that 90% of normal behavior is due to habits! Being and staying organized is all about creating consistent work habits. Here are some ways to help you continue the momentum for change:

- **Just do it**—There are so many reasons, challenges, and barriers to avoid changing organizational habits. Even change that we know is good for us is hard to effect. Take one day at a time and just do it!

- **Set realistic expectations for yourself**—You are not going to be able to change everything all at once. Start with one item you want to change, develop that habit, and then work on the next process change.

- **Develop consistency**—Repetition helps immensely when you're trying to develop a new habit. If one day you don't do a particular task that you're trying to make a habit, do your best to integrate it in the following day. The more repetitive work and organizational processes become, the less you will have to think about doing them.

- **Ask for support from your colleagues, spouse, or friends**—Tell them what you want to change and ask them to remind or follow up with you about it periodically. This breeds accountability with change and helps you to keep your own commitments. Others also can be a nice motivational cheerleading squad for you!

- **Get back on track if you get out of the habit**—There will always be certain circumstances (travel, all-day meetings, and so on) that cause you to get out of your organizational habits and processes. Avoid feeling guilty or becoming overwhelmed when those circumstances happen. Just get back on track and begin the next day with your work processes and organization.

Minimizing Interruptions

Some interruptions are necessary and even vital in certain environments and with certain jobs. Everyone has a unique perception of what constitutes an interruption. Phone calls, email, people stopping by your office—anything that takes you away from your task at hand—are interruptions. Statistics say that it takes approximately 20 minutes to get back to the level of concentration you were at before an interruption occurred. If you don't want interruptions to control your day, you need to develop your own plan for minimizing them.

Consider tracking your interruptions for a week or so to determine the type of interruptions you receive daily. Create a spreadsheet or use your day planner to track the date and time, the interrupter, the topic or questions asked, and the length of time spent. After one week, analyze the data and consider the following questions:

- Did certain individuals interrupt you more than others?
- Did most interruptions occur during specific time intervals?
- Were the interruption topics or questions appropriate for you to answer, given your job title?
- What were the most frequent types of interruptions? Individuals who were socializing? Colleagues who needed decisions or information from you?
- What was the average length of time you spent with each interruption? How much total time in the week did the interruptions take?

Use the information from your tracking document to determine the amount of time you're losing to interruptions and to develop a plan to deal with the worst offenders.

With every interruption, you have a choice of the following:

- Deal with the question, answer it, and take action accordingly.
- Defer the interruption and request another time to discuss it.
- Forward the interrupter to another person to deal with the issue or request.
- Encourage others to devise their own solutions and manage the issue on their own.

Deferring Interruptions

If you are working on something that is a priority and want to defer interruptions, or if the interruption is not immediate in nature, you should request a deferral of the interruption.

Here are some sample phrases you can use:

"I'd love to help you; let me finish what I'm doing and get back to you."

"Could we discuss this later this afternoon?"

"Could we discuss this at our next meeting or appointment?"

If you have certain colleagues who regularly need your guidance, consider planning a consistent time with them to answer questions. Having a designated time will encourage you to listen better and encourage the person to hold his questions to your meeting time.

Have your assistant, if you have one, serve as a door manager to help reduce interruptions. Your assistant should be located near your office and be the first person the individuals

> **tip** If you do find yourself interrupted in the middle of a task, write a quick reminder to yourself about what and where you left off. Note it on the document itself, in your day planner, or in your notepad. That way, you have a reminder of where to begin when you return.

speak with before coming to you. The assistant can determine the necessity of the interruption. If the interruption could wait, the assistant should ask the interrupter to return at a later time or schedule a time with him to meet you later.

Using Nonverbal Language to Minimize Interruptions

It can be difficult to defer some interruptions or ask that person to go away. There are some subtle, but effective, nonverbal things you can do to help minimize interruptions:

- **Put your briefcase or bag in the empty chair near your desk**—This discourages anyone from sitting down and getting comfortable, which increases the length of interruptions.

- **Stand up when someone enters your office**—The interrupter will be less inclined to sit down and more inclined to communicate directly and quickly.

- **Walk the interrupter to your door or entrance to your cubicle**—This is another nonverbal signal of closing your conversation and making it less comfortable for the interrupter to continue.

- **Ask to go to the other person's office to speak**—This way, you have more control of when to leave.

- **Create two areas in your office**—Create one that is visible from the doorway, which you can use when you don't mind being interrupted, and another area that's not visible, which you can use when you do not want to be interrupted. If you do this, you might want to get a laptop so you can work in both areas.

- **Close the door to your office**—If you have a door, use it! Close the door when you need to concentrate or focus. If you need to, place a sign on the door and ask individuals to come back at a designated time when the door will be opened again.

> **tip** Consider creating certain time periods of the day that your door is always closed. Then others will learn when they can come talk with you.

- **Face away from the door or traffic**—Move your computer or desk so you minimize eye contact with passersby.

- **Create a sign or symbols to indicate you are not available**—If someone interrupts you while your sign is up, you will have to ask him to come back at a later time and reinforce your signal. CubeDoor is a product that is retractable cubicle door that is great for minimizing interruptions in cubicle office environments. To order CubeDoor go to www.cubedoor.com.

Avoiding Interruptions

In some jobs and office environments, it is hard to avoid all interruptions, but here are some ways to avoid certain types:

- **Work outside the office**—If technology and your work demands permit it, work from home one day or morning a week. Or, go to a coffee or tea shop that has wireless access.

- **Refrain from answering the phone**—During your "uninterruption" work blocks, let calls go to voice mail.

- **Refrain from checking email more than two or three times daily**—Refrain from checking email constantly. It is as much an interrupter as people walking into your office.

- **Change your work hours**—Come earlier or stay one hour later than normal work hours. If your colleagues are not in the office, there is less likelihood they will interrupt you!

- **Establish a time limit with the interrupter when the interruption begins**—You can say, "I only have a few minutes; what can I help you with?" or "I am working on something that requires my full attention; can we handle this in 2 minutes or less?"

note Goethe once said, "Things which matter most must never be at the mercy of things which matter least." Minimize interruptions during the work day so you can concentrate your time on the most important projects and action items to be accomplished. And remember—one of the most effective ways to control interruptions is to avoid being an interrupter yourself.

HOME OFFICE INTERRUPTIONS

Many people who work in their home offices find it difficult to make a clear distinction between work time and nonwork time. Communicate with your family and friends about the best times to interrupt or call you during the work day. If you haven't already, sign up for caller ID; this will help you prioritize incoming calls, as well as minimize interruptions from solicitors during the day. Finally, be sure you have a nonwork life—stop your business day at a reasonable and consistent hour each day. Then your family and friends can be guaranteed a time to contact you after work.

To do list

- ☐ Avoid picking up the phone when you are in the middle of doing something important.
- ☐ Determine a method to track incoming phone calls and voice mails.
- ☐ Return phone calls during one time frame, and be clear and concise when leaving voice mail messages.
- ☐ Avoid unnecessarily long phone calls, and establish time limits before beginning a conversation.

Maximizing Phone Time

As with email, the phone is a standard communication method that needs to be managed and organized appropriately. Phone calls, as with email, can take up more precious time than you have. It is important to devise a method and a designated time in your schedule for tracking and responding to your phone calls and voice mails. Controlling your phone time can help you maximize your work time when you need it most.

Answering the Phone

Some individuals are in the habit of picking up the telephone when it rings, no matter what they are doing or who they are talking to. Often, we do that from habit, rather than because we fear we'll miss an important call. However, if you are working on an important project, you make better use of your time by letting some calls go to voice mail and dealing with them later.

Often we are not in a situation to talk with the caller and have to defer the call or conversation anyway. Be more conscious of when you answer the phone if you are in a position to deal with the call itself.

You shouldscreen calls through your caller ID or your receptionist or assistant. Ask others to request more specifics of what the caller needs and provide them with a list of frequently asked questions. Sometimes, they can give the caller what she needs without the call being transferred to you.

tip
If you work from home, reduce your telemarketing calls by registering with the National Do Not Call Registry at www.donotcall.gov. After you register your name and home or mobile telephone numbers, you are automatically on the list for 5 years. This should stop all telemarketing calls from companies with which you have not had a prior business relationship.

Tracking Phone Calls and Messages

Develop a method to track your phone calls and voice mail messages. Having one call list to refer to makes returning calls and dealing with issues easier. Refrain from using sticky notes and small pieces of paper, which seem to get lost or buried. Here are some methods you can use to track phone calls and voice mail messages:

- **Use a separate spiral notebook**—Be sure to date the top of each page, so you can refer to it if needed. Keep the notebook near your phone for easy access. When the notebook is full, you can write the date range on the front of it and save it for a period of time.

- **Use your daily pages in your day planner**—Use the opposite side in a two-page-per-day view of your day planner. Or, create a separate tab and section solely to track voice mail messages.

- **Type the messages in a Word document**—Put the current phone messages at the top rather than the bottom for easier access. Create a new document after a week or month of calls.

- **Create a calendar entry each day in your contact manager**—Type in the subject line **today's phone calls**, and type all the voice mail messages in the notes field. This way, you have a chronological history in your calendar of the calls you received each day.

- **Consider using email as a substitute for taking phone messages**—Use the subject line to write who called, the phone number, and the issue. Then, you can respond to the person via email. Responding via email also enables you to have a written record of the communication, if needed.

- **Use specific telephone messaging software**—A few voice mail software systems are While You Were Out (www.caliente.com) and PhonePad (www.cyber-com-software.com/phonepadoverview.htm). Both enable you to take phone messages electronically and to search and organize by the caller's name, the date, or the phone number. You can also send electronic telephone messages to other users if you are on a networked system.

- **Use voice mail messaging software**—Voice mail messaging software enables your computer to answer and record the voice mail for you. EzVoice (www.internetsoftsolution.com) is voice mail software that is available for less than $30. You can record customized greetings for different individuals. EzVoice allows you to take additional notes per each voice mail message it records.

Calling When the Time Is Right

When you are ready to return calls, try to do most of your calling during a single time period. The best times to return calls are first thing in the morning, right after lunch, and during the last two hours of the day. Most people are in their offices then, which reduces the likelihood that you'll get caught in phone tag.

If you are not able to reach someone, consider setting a telephone appointment. To avoid telephone tag, let the person know the best time to reach you in your office or on your cell phone. Leave as much information as you can of exactly what you need and when you need it by. This allows the return caller to leave the answer on your voice mail and hopefully resolve the question or issue without too many voice mail messages.

Before you call, or return the call, take a few moments to think about what you need and whether the person you are calling has all the data he needs to respond to you. Would it be better to address the issue via email? This is especially helpful if you need to give the person information he most likely will need to think about or give some thought to before he responds.

We all hate those rambling voice mail messages where we are not sure what the caller really wants. When leaving voice mail messages, be specific and to the point. Be sure to leave key information in the beginning of your message, such as your name, the date, the time, and your phone number. Then, let the person know what you want and the best way to reach you. Consider leaving your email address on the voice mail to give the person the option to email you his response.

VOICE MAIL GREETINGS

It is as important to leave a clear voice mail greeting as it is to leave a good voice mail message. When recording your greeting, give the following information:

- **Bypass options**—Most phone systems have bypass options of skipping the greeting to go directly into voice mail. Let callers know in the beginning how to perform this bypass function.

- **Information you need**—List the information you would like callers to leave. This makes it clear what you need to return the call and is a good reminder to people calling in a hurry to leave you all the information you need.

- **Best times to reach you**—Give callers the best times to reach you in your office. Also, let them know the times you usually return phone calls. This information lets the caller know when to expect a return phone call.

- **Alternative methods to reach you**—With so many communication devices, let callers know the best way to reach you. Maybe that is your cell phone, email, your home phone, or through your assistant.

- **Name and method of alternative contact**—If you are in an office setting, give callers an option to reach a live person if you are not available. This could be a colleague, your assistant, or the company operator.

Avoiding Unnecessarily Long Phone Calls

If you're not calling to catch up or have a friendly chat, you probably need to keep work day calls brief and to the point. Here are things you can do to set the stage for a brief phone call instead of a long one:

- **Say "I hope you are well" instead of "How are you?"**—When you begin the conversation with a question, you can expect an answer. If you start the conversation with a statement, though, you still give the impression of concern without getting the long answer you hope to avoid.

- **Establish a time limit up front**—Begin with "I only have a few minutes till my next meeting" (whether you have one or not). Or let the other person know that you have only a few minutes and ask her what she needs. This sets the stage for a brief conversation.

- **Write down what you want to accomplish**—Especially if you have a few items you need to discuss with someone, write a list of what you want to review. This helps you and the recipient stay on track.

- **Set a timer**—If you find that you are the guilty party with long phone calls, use a timer and set it for a reasonable amount of time for the phone call. When it rings, that's your cue to wrap up the conversation.

Summary

Each individual, job, and organization is different and requires a different organizational system to be, and stay, organized. Throughout this book, I have given you a multitude of options of ways in which you can be more productive and efficient in managing your information, communications, tasks, and time. It is important for you to determine which system or process will work best for you. Determine which areas are the biggest time-wasters or challenges in your work day, and develop your own organizational plan based on some of the recommendations in this book.

You can create all the systems you want, but if you don't follow through with them, you will be stuck with the same habits you had before you read this book. Be cautious of trying to change all your work systems at once. Pick one or two new systems that will bring the most value and productivity to your work life, and create those to become habits. Don't get discouraged if you can't have every aspect in your office organized right now. Tackle one area at a time and get accustomed to your new system so it becomes habit and you feel in control. Then, tackle the next challenging area.

We all have our own excuses for not getting things done—and that list can be long! It is important to plan your day, manage your procrastination habits, and have a plan to deal with interruptions as they occur. Doing this in conjunction with organizing your data and information creates an effective and productive work day. In this chapter you learned about

- How to plan your day
- Managing your schedule and interruptions
- Tracking and managing incoming and outgoing telephone calls

References and Resources

This appendix is a list of resources that will be helpful to you on your journey to becoming more efficient and productive in your work life. Some of the resources listed here are referenced in this book but have been consolidated in this appendix for your convenience. This appendix also contains a glossary of technical terms used in the book.

Organizing Associations and Organizations

The following are associations and organizations where you can find leading organizing consultants and professionals:

> **note** A full listing of all the online sources recommended in this book is located on our website at www.quepublishing.com under the ISBN.

- **Clutterless Recovery Groups (www. clutter-recovery.com)**—An organization that provides support groups across the country to help individuals who are prone to clutter.

- **Independent Computer Consultants Association (www.icca.org)**—An organization that can help locate a computer consultant in your area.

- **National Association of Professional Organizers (www.napo.net)**—An organization of consultants who help others with organization, efficiency, and productivity. To find a consultant in your area, click the Find an Organizer link.
- **National Study Group on Chronic Disorganization (www.nsgcd.org)**—An organization that offers referrals and assistance to anyone interested in or seeking help for chronic disorganization.

Suggested Reading and Viewing List

So many books, so little time! There are many wonderful books on organization, time management, and business efficiency. I listed only a few that I hope will provide you with some different perspectives and outlooks from those I've offered in this book. I hope you find them useful.

General Organization

Numerous books on organization are now available, each with its own flavor and specialization. Here is a list of some of the leading publications on organization:

- *Conquering Chronic Disorganization* by Judith Kolberg (Squall Press, Inc., 1999)—Ms. Kolberg is one of the leading specialists on chronic disorganization. Her book gives innovative and creative ideas on nontraditional organizing techniques.
- *Organized for Success* by Stephanie Winston (Crown Business, 2004)—A book with anecdotes from leading company executives, it provides organizational tips and tricks the executives use.
- *Organizing from the Inside Out* by Julie Morgenstern (Owl Books, 1999)—A great book that discusses the philosophy of getting and staying organized.
- *Taming the Office Tiger* by Barbara Hemphill (Kiplinger, 1996)—A very practical how-to book on organizing your office.

Time Management

Following is a list of some other time-management products that focus on a different areas and topics:

- *Getting Things Done* by David Allen (Penguin Books, 2001)—A fantastic book that discusses in length how to break down tasks and make them manageable.

- *How to Be Organized in Spite of Yourself* by Sunny Schlenger (New American, 1999)—A book that describes various organizational habits and matches them with a variety of personality styles.

- *Mission Control Productivity and Accomplishment Video* (Mission Control Productivity, Inc., 2003)—This video discusses the development of work habits and how to change them.

- *The Path: Creating Your Mission Statement for Work and for Life* by Laurie Beth Jones (Hyperion, 1996)—This book discusses how to create a personal mission statement.

- *The Seven Habits of Highly Effective People* by Stephen R. Covey (Free Press, 1990) and *First Things First* by Stephen R. Covey, A. Roger Merrill, and Rebecca R. Merrill (Simon & Schuster, 1994)—These are both classic time-management books that focus on using your time to support and develop your values and goals.

- *Take Back Your Time Day* by John De Graaf (Berrett Koehler, 2003)—A compilation of writings by authors who discuss the issue of overworked Americans and how to change the paradigm.

General Business

Both of these books are business classics:

- *Getting to Yes* by William Ury (Penguin Books, 1991)—A classic book on negotiation that teaches basic skills on how to negotiate. A great tool to use, especially when negotiating time commitments.

- *Good to Great* by Jim Collins (Harper Business, 2001)—Mr. Collins did 5 years of research on the best companies in America and the aspects that made them great. A terrific book on what to start, and stop, doing in your work life.

Other Books

These are other resources that I mentioned throughout this book:

- *The Cult of Information: The Folklore of Computers and the True Art of Thinking* by Theodore Roszak (Lutterworth Publishers, 1986)

- *Data Smog: Surviving the Information Glut* by David Shenk (Harper, 1997)

Technology Glossary

The world of computer technology has a language of its own! Following is a list of computer terminology used in this book that you might find helpful to reference. For definitions not located in this glossary, refer to Webopedia (www.webopedia.com) or TechWeb (www.techweb.com), which are online encyclopedias for computer technology terms.

backup   A secondary location of original data. A backup can be stored on external media, such as CD-ROM or DVD-ROM, or another interal or external hard drive.

CD-ROM   A type of disc media that can store data and is commonly used for recording music or computer files. This disc is read-only, and the data cannot be manipulated after it's recorded onto the CD.

CD-RW   A similar media to CD-ROM, except that after data has been recorded, it is *rewritable*. This means the data on the CD can be saved, or written, over.

contact management software   Software that is specifically designed to manage contact information. This software usually also performs the functions of calendar, task list, and email communications.

cookie   A file automatically stored on a user's hard drive, it is created by website servers to remember the user and his preferences when he returns to the website.

customer relationship manager (CRM)   Software that is designed to manage a large volume (over 5,000) of contacts; it's primarily used in sales industries.

desktop   The operating system's working area screen that holds icons for shortcuts, programs, and files stored on the computer.

drop-down button/arrow   An onscreen feature included in many types of software that enables you to display a list of options that accompany a command. It is most commonly used with a state-based field, where when you click in the field, a drop-down list of states appears.

DVD   A disc media that is similar to the CD-ROM but holds a larger amount of data (up to 5GB). It is most commonly used for recording movies and to back up hard drives.

Ethernet   A cord that is a little bigger than a standard telephone cord and is used to transfer data between equipment. It is most commonly used to network computers and connect to the Internet.

file allocation table (FAT)   The FAT directs where files are to be stored and accessed on the hard drive. It is commonly used to describe the type of file system on a computer.

floppy disk   A type of disk medium that is 3 1/2" square in size. It can store up to 1.4MB of memory. This was the standard disk medium used to carry and store data from computers before the CD-ROM was developed.

freeware   Software that is available on the Internet to download for free.

gigabyte (GB)   A computer measurement of information equal to 1,073,741,824 bytes. Gigabytes usually refer to the size of a computer hard drive.

handheld   A common term used to describe the small, handheld devices such as PDAs. Popular handhelds are Palm Pilot, Treo, and BlackBerry.

hard drive   A card-type device that reads and writes a large amount of data that is usually stored inside your computer (although removable hard drives are becoming more common). The hard drive is commonly where software programs and electronic documents are stored inside your computer.

Internet   An international network of computers that provides access to data and information. To gain access to the Internet, you must have an Internet service provider.

ISP   An acronym for Internet service provider, which is a service that provides access to the Internet and World Wide Web.

IT (information technology)   Relates to the management of information within technology systems. IT is most commonly referred to as the computer department within a company or an organization.

kilobyte (KB)   A computer measurement of information equal to 1,024 bytes. This measurement is commonly used to describe the size of electronic documents and files.

Mac (Macintosh)   A type of computer produced by Apple Computers. This was the first computer to introduce the window and mouse technology. It is the computer most widely used in schools and marketing and graphic arts industries.

media   A data storage device; this term most commonly refers to portable media such as CD-ROM, DVD, jump drives, and tapes.

megabyte (MB)   A computer measurement of information equal to 1,048,576 bytes. This measurement is typically used to describe the size of media and large graphic files.

operating system   An underlying program that operates the basic functions on a computer and enables software programs to run.

optical character recognition (OCR)   Software technology that translates scanned characters into readable text. The software is commonly used for document scanning.

personal computer (PC)   Generally, a computer equipped with a Microsoft Windows-based operating system and software.

personal digital assistant (PDA)   A small, handheld device that syncs with a contact manager or personal information manager and typically can be used as a phone, fax sender, web browser, and personal data organizer.

personal information manager (PIM)   A type of software that is used as an electronic time-management tool. The software is an all-in-one tool that tracks an individual's appointments, tasks, contacts, notes, and email. The most commonly used PIM today is Microsoft Outlook.

Portable Document Format (PDF)   A document format developed by Adobe Systems, it enables a document to be viewed by others in its original form, without needing to have the original software in which it was produced. A PDF document can be opened only with Adobe Acrobat Reader, which is available free from the Adobe website (www.adobe.com).

RAM   An acronym for random access memory. This is referred to as *short-term memory* because the data is forgotten after the computer or other device is turned off. This is the memory typically used with printers and operating programs on your computer.

reboot   The function performed to restart the computer.

ROM   An acronym for read-only memory. This is referred to as *hard drive memory* and is the permanent memory of a computer. With ROM, you can turn off the computer and it retains the data and does not erase it.

scanning   The electronic process of using a scanning device to create an electronic file that contains a reproduction of a paper-based document. Most copy machines function as scanners.

server   A computer that acts as a master computer and is the one computer that manages a network of computers. A server usually has a very large hard drive and is the main storage device for a company's data.

shareware   Trial-based software that can be downloaded for free, initially. If the user decides to continue using the software, she must pay a small fee and register.

shortcut   A type of file that points to another file or document stored in another location on a computer. Shortcuts are most commonly used on the desktop to quickly open files and programs.

spam   Unsolicited email that is the electronic version of paper junk mail. Spam email is generally used for marketing purposes and sent to a large volume of email recipients.

sync   An abbreviated term meaning the act of synchronization between two computers or programs. When synchronization is performed, the computers exchange data so that both files will be exactly the same.

third-party software   Software developed to interact with operating systems or software designed by other manufacturers.

Universal Serial Bus (USB)   A standard type of connector used to plug removable devices into a computer.

USB jump drive   A popular keychain-type of data storage device that plugs into the computer using a USB port. This type of storage device does not require a driver or software to use it.

virus   A program distributed from computer to computer via the Internet for the purpose of harming the computers' operation. The program is usually an attachment to an email that is not a recognized type of file or document. The attachment must be opened or launched for the virus to become active in your computer.

window   Refers to the functionality on your computer that opens another program or shows a different set of data on your screen. With today's technology, multiple windows can be displayed on a computer screen.

Wireless-Fidelity (Wi-Fi)   A wireless method of connecting to the Internet or other computers.

wireless Internet service provider (WISP)   A company that provides service to the Internet without the use of telephone or Ethernet cords, by using wireless technology.

Index

Do Even More ...In No Time

Must See

Get ready to cross off those items on your to-do list! *In No Time* helps you tackle the projects that you don't think you have time to finish. With shopping lists and step-by-step instructions, these books get you working toward accomplishing your goals.

Check out these other *In No Time* books, coming soon!

Start Your Own Home Business In No Time
ISBN: **0-7897-3224-6**
$16.95
September 2004

Plan a Fabulous Party In No Time
ISBN: **0-7897-3221-1**
$16.95
September 2004

Speak Basic Spanish In No Time
ISBN: **0-7897-3223-8**
$16.95
September 2004

Organize Your Garage In No Time
ISBN: **0-7897-3219-X**
$16.95
October 2004

Quick Family Meals In No Time
ISBN: **0-7897-3299-8**
$16.95
October 2004

Organize Your Family's Schedule In No Time
ISBN: **0-7897-3220-3**
$16.95
October 2004